The Freedom of Life

*A*nnie *P*ayson *C*all

Writat

This edition published in 2021

ISBN : 9789390439423

Design and Setting By
Writat
(An Imprint of Vij Publishiing Group)
www.vijbooks.in
contact@vijpublishing.com

Contents

FREEDOM

LORD GOD of Israel,—
Where Thou art we are free!
Call out Thy people, Lord, we pray,
From Egypt unto Thee.
Open our eyes that we may see
Our bondage in the past,—
Oh, help us, Lord, to keep Thy law,
And make us free at last!

Lord God of Israel,—
Where Thou art we are free!
Freed from the rule of alien minds,
We turn our hearts to Thee.
The alien hand weighs heavily,
And heavy is our sin,—
Thy children cry to Thee, O Lord,—
Their God,—to take them in.

Lord God of Israel,—
Where Thou 'art we are free
Cast down our idols from on high,
That we may worship Thee.
In freedom we will live Thy Love
Out from our inmost parts;
Upon our foreheads bind Thy Law,—
Engrave it on our hearts!

Amen.

INTRODUCTION

INTERIOR freedom rests upon the principle of non-resistance to all the things which seem evil or painful to our natural love of self. But non-resistance alone can accomplish nothing good unless, behind it, there is a strong love for righteousness and truth. By refusing to resist the ill will of others, or the stress of circumstances, for the sake of greater usefulness and a clearer point of view, we deepen our conviction of righteousness as the fundamental law of fife, and broaden our horizon so as to appreciate varying and opposite points of view. The only non-resistance that brings this power is the kind which yields mere personal and selfish considerations for the sake of principles. Selfish and weak yielding must always do harm. Unselfish yielding, on the other hand, strengthens the will and increases strength of purpose as the petty obstacles of mere self-love are removed. Concentration alone cannot long remain wholesome, for it needs the light of growing self-knowledge to prevent its becoming self-centred. Yielding alone is of no avail, for in itself it has no constructive power. But if we try to look at ourselves as we really are, we shall find great strength in yielding where only our small and private interests are concerned, and concentrating upon living the broad principles of righteousness which must directly or indirectly affect all those with whom we come into contact.

I.
The Freedom of Life

I AM so tired I must give up work," said a young woman with a very strained and tearful face; and it seemed to her a desperate state, for she was dependent upon work for her bread and butter. If she gave up work she gave up bread and butter, and that meant starvation. When she was asked why she did not keep at work and learn to do it without getting so tired, that seemed to her absurd, and she would have laughed if laughing had been possible.

"I tell you the work has tired me so that I cannot stand it, and you ask me to go back and get rest out of it when I am ready to die of fatigue. Why don't you ask me to burn myself, on a piece of ice, or freeze myself with a red-hot poker?"

"But," the answer was, "it is not the work that tires you at all, it is the way you do it;" and, after a little soothing talk which quieted the overexcited nerves, she began to feel a dawning intelligence, which showed her that, after all, there might be life in the work which she had come to look upon as nothing but slow and painful death. She came to understand that she might do her work as if she were working very lazily, going from one thing to another with a feeling as near to entire indifference as she could cultivate, and, at the same time, do it well. She was shown by illustrations how she might walk across the room and take a book off the table as if her life depended upon it, racing and pushing over the floor, grabbing the book and clutching it until she got back to her seat, or, how she might move with exaggerated laziness take the book up loosely, and drag herself back again. This illustration represents two extremes, and one, in itself, is as bad as the other; but, when the habit has been one of unnecessary strain and effort, the lazy way, practised for a time, will not only be very restful, but will eventually lead to movement which is quick as well.

To take another example, you may write holding the pen with much more force than is needful, tightening your throat and tongue at the same time, or you may drag your pen along the paper and relieve the tendency to tension in your throat and tongue by opening your mouth slightly and letting your jaw hang loosely. These again are two extremes, but, if the habit has been one of tension, a persistent practice of the extreme of looseness will lead to a quiet mode of writing in which ten pages can be finished with the effort it formerly took to write one.

Sometimes the habit of needless strain has taken such a strong hold that the very effort to work quietly seems so unnatural as to cause much nervous suffering. To turn the corner from a bad habit into a true and wholesome one is often very painful, but, the first pain worked through, the right habit grows more and more easy, until finally the better way carries us along and we take it involuntarily.

For the young woman who felt she had come to the end of her powers, it was work or die; therefore, when she had become rested enough to see and understand at all, she welcomed the idea that it was not her work that tired her, but the way in which she did it, and she listened eagerly to the directions that should teach her to do it with less fatigue, and, as an experiment, offered to go back and try the "lazy way" for a week. At the end of a week she reported that the "lazy way" had rested her remarkably, but she did not do her work so well. Then she had to learn that she could keep more quietly and steadily concentrated upon her work, doing it accurately and well, without in the least interfering with the "lazy way." Indeed, the better concentrated we are, the more easily and restfully we can work, for concentration does not mean straining every nerve and muscle toward our work,—it means *dropping everything that interferes,* and strained nerves and muscles constitute a very bondage of interference.

The young woman went back to her work for another week's experiment, and this time returned with a smiling face, better color, and a new and more quiet life in her eyes. She had made the "lazy way" work, and found a better power of concentration at the same time. She knew that it was only a beginning, but she felt secure now in the certain knowledge that it was not her work that had been killing her, but the way in which she had done it; and she felt confident of her power to do it restfully and, at the same time, better than before. Moreover, in addition to practising the new way of working, she planned to get regular exercise in the open air, even if it had to come in the evening, and to eat only nourishing food. She has been at work now for several years, and, at last accounts, was still busy, with no temptation to stop because of overfatigue.

If any reader is conscious of suffering now from the strain of his work and would like to get relief, the first thing to do is to notice that it is less the work that tires him than his way of doing it, and the attitude of his mind toward it. Beginning with that conviction, there comes at first an interest in the process of dropping strain and then a new interest in the work itself, and a healthy concentration in doing the merest drudgery as well as it can be done, makes the drudgery attractive and relieves one from the oppressive fatigue of uninteresting monotony.

If you have to move your whole body in your daily work, the first care should be to move the feet and legs heavily. Feel as if each foot weighed a ton, and each hand also; and while you work take long, quiet breaths,—breaths such as you see a man taking when he is very quietly and soundly sleeping.

If the work is sedentary, it is a help before starting in the morning to drop your head forward very loosely, slowly and heavily, and raise it very slowly, then take a long, quiet breath. Repeat this several times until you begin to feel a sense of weight in your head. If there is not time in the morning, do it at night and recall the feeling while you are dressing or while you are going to work, and then, during your work, stop occasionally just to feel your head heavy and then go on. Very soon you become sensitive to the tension in the back of your neck and drop it without stopping work at all.

Long, quiet breaths while you work are always helpful. If you are working in bad air, and cannot change the air, it is better to try to have the breaths only quiet and gentle, and take long, full breaths whenever you are out-of-doors and before going to sleep at night.

Of course, a strained way of working is only one cause of nervous fatigue; there are others, and even more important ones, that need to be understood in order that we may be freed from the bondage of nervous strain which keeps so many of us from our best use and happiness.

Many people are in bondage because of doing wrong, but many more because of doing right in the wrong way. Real freedom is only found through obedience to law, and when, because of daily strain, a man finds himself getting overtired and irritable, the temptation is to think it easier to go on working in the wrong way than to make the effort to learn how to work in the right way. At first the effort seems only to result in extra strain, but, if persisted in quietly, it soon becomes apparent that it is leading to less and less strain, and finally to restful work.

There are laws for rest, laws for work, and laws for play, which, if we find and follow them, lead us to quiet, useful lines of life, which would be impossible without them. They are the laws of our own being, and should carry us as naturally as the instincts of the animals carry them, and so enable us to do right in the right way, and make us so sure of the manner in which we do our work that we can give all our attention to the work itself; and when we have the right habit of working, the work itself must necessarily gain, because we can put the best of ourselves into it.

It is helpful to think of the instincts of the beasts, how true and orderly they are, on their own plane, and how they are only perverted when the animals have come under the influence of man. Imagine Baloo, the bear in Mr. Kipling's "Jungle Book," being asked how he managed to keep so well and rested. He would look a little surprised and say: "Why, I follow the laws of my being. How could I do differently?" Now that is just the difference between man and beast. Man can do differently. And man has done differently now for so many generations that not one in ten thousand really recognizes what the laws of his being are, except in ways so gross that it seems as if we had sunken to the necessity of being guided by a crowbar, instead of steadily following the delicate instinct which is ours by right, and so voluntarily accepting the guidance of the Power who made us, which is the only possible way to freedom.

Of course the laws of a man's being are infinitely above the laws of a beast's. The laws of a man's being are spiritual, and the animal in man is meant to be the servant of his soul. Man's true guiding instincts are in his soul,—he can obey them or not, as he chooses; but the beast's instincts are in his body, and he has no choice but to obey. Man can, so to speak, get up and look down on himself. He can be his own father and his own mother. From his true instinct he can say to himself, "you must do this" or "You must not do that." He can see and understand his tendency to disobedience, and *he can force himself to obey.* Man can see the good and wholesome animal instincts in himself that lead to lasting health and strength, and he can make them all the good servants of his soul. He can see the tendency to overindulgence, and how it leads to disease and to evil, and he can refuse to permit that wrong tendency to rule him.

Every man has his own power of distinguishing between right and wrong, and his own power of choosing which way he shall follow. He is left free to choose God's way or to choose his own. Through past and present perversions, of natural habit he has lost the delicate power of distinguishing the normal from the abnormal, and needs to be educated back to it. The benefit of this education is an intelligent consciousness of the laws of life, which not only adds to his own strength of mind and body, but increases immeasurably his power of use to others. Many customs of to-day fix and perpetuate abnormal habits to such an extent that, combined with our own selfish inheritances and personal perversions, they dim the light of our minds so that many of us are working all the time in a fog, more or less dense, of ignorance and bondage. When a man chooses the right and refuses the wrong, in so far as he sees it, he becomes wise from within and from without, his power for distinguishing gradually improves, the fog lifts, and he finds within himself a sure and delicate instinct which was formerly atrophied for want of use.

The first thing to understand without the shadow of a doubt, is that, man is not in freedom when he is following his own selfish instincts. He is only in the appearance of freedom, and the appearance of freedom, without the reality, leads invariably to the worst bondage. A man who loves drink feels that he is free if he can drink as much as he wants, but that leads to degradation and delirium tremens. A man who has an inherited tendency toward the disobedience of any law feels that he is free if he has the opportunity to disobey it whenever he wants to. But whatever the law may be, the results have only to be carried to their logical conclusion to make clear the bondage to which the disobedience leads. All this disobedience to law leads to an inevitable, inflexible, unsurmountable limit in the end, whereas steady effort toward obedience to law is unlimited in its development of strength and power for use to others. Man must understand his selfish tendencies in order to subdue and control them, until they become subject to his own unselfish tendencies, which are the spiritual laws within him. Thus he gradually becomes free,—soul and body,—with no desire to disobey, and with steadily increasing joy in his work and life. So much for the bondage of doing wrong, and the freedom of doing right, which it seems necessary to touch upon, in order to show clearly the bondage of doing right in the wrong way, and the freedom of doing right in the right way.

It is right to work for our daily bread, and for the sake of use to others, in whatever form it may present itself. The wrong way of doing it makes unnecessary strain, overfatigue and illness. The right way of working gives, as we have said before, new power and joy in the work; it often turns even drudgery into pleasure, for there is a special delight in learning to apply one's self in a true spirit to "drudgery." The process of learning such true application of one's powers often reveals new possibilities in work.

It is right for most people to sleep eight hours every night. The wrong way of doing it is to go to sleep all doubled up, and to continue to work all night in our sleep, instead of giving up and resting entirely. The right way gives us the fullest possible amount of rest and refreshment.

It is right to take our three meals a day, and all the nourishing food we need. The wrong way of doing it, is to eat very fast, without chewing our food carefully, and to give our stomachs no restful opportunity of preparation to receive its food, or to take good care of it after it is received. The right way gives us the opportunity to assimilate the food entirely, so that every bit of fuel we put into our bodies is burnt to some good purpose, and makes us more truly ready to receive more.

It is right to play and amuse ourselves for rest and recreation. We play in the wrong way when we use ourselves up in the strain of playing, in the anxiety lest we should not win in a game, or when we play in bad air. When we play in the right way, there is no strain, no anxiety, only good fun and refreshment and rest.

We might go through the narrative of an average life in showing briefly the wonderful difference between doing right in the right way, and doing right in the wrong way. It is not too much to say that the difference in tendency is as great as that between life and death.

It is one thing to read about orderly living and to acknowledge that the ways described are good and true, and quite another to have one's eyes opened and to act from the new knowledge, day by day, until a normal mode of life is firmly established. It requires quiet, steady force of will to get one's self out of bad, and well established in good habits. After the first interest and relief there often has to be steady plodding before the new way becomes easy; but if we do not allow ourselves to get discouraged, we are sure to gain our end, for we are opening ourselves to the influence of the true laws within us, and in finding and obeying these we are approaching the only possible Freedom of Life.

II.
How to Sleep Restfully

IT would seem that at least one might be perfectly free in sleep. But the habits of cleaving to mistaken ways of living cannot be thrown off at night and taken up again in the morning. They go to sleep with us and they wake with us.

If, however, we learn better habits of sleeping, that helps us in our life through the day. And learning better habits through the day helps us to get more rest from our sleep. At the end of a good day we can settle down more quickly to get ready for sleep, and, when we wake in the morning, find ourselves more ready to begin the day to come.

There are three things that prevent sleep,—overfatigue, material disturbances from the outside, and mental disturbances from, within.

It is not uncommon to hear people say, "I was too tired to sleep"—but it is not generally known how great a help it is at such times not to try to sleep, but to go to work deliberately to get I rested in preparation for it. In nine cases out of ten it is the unwillingness to lie awake that keeps us awake. We wonder why we do not sleep. We toss and turn and wish we could sleep. We fret, and fume, and worry, because we do not sleep. We think of all we have to do on the following day, and are oppressed with the thought that we cannot do it if we do not sleep. First, we try one experiment to see if it will not make us sleep, and when it fails, we try another, and perhaps another. In each experiment we, are watching to see if it will work. There are many things to do, any one of which might help us to sleep, but the *watching to see if they will work keeps us awake.*

When we are kept awake from our fatigue, the first thing to do is to say over and over to ourselves that we do not care whether we sleep or not, in order to imbue ourselves with a healthy indifference about it. It will help toward gaining this wholesome indifference to say "I am too tired to sleep, and therefore, the first thing for me to do is to get rested in order to prepare for sleep. When my brain is well rested, it will go to sleep; it cannot help it. When it is well rested, it will sleep just as naturally as my lungs breathe, or as my heart beats."

In order to rest our brains we want to lie quietly, relaxing all our muscles, and taking even, quiet breaths. It is good when we can take long, full breaths, but sometimes that is too fatiguing; and then we must not only take moderately long, breaths, but be careful to have them gentle, quiet, and rhythmic. To make a plan of breathing and follow it keeps the mind steadily concentrated on the breathing, and gives the rest of the brain, which has been working on other things, a chance to relax and find its own freedom and rest. It is helpful to inhale while we count seven, exhale while we count seven, then rest and breathe naturally while we count seven, and to repeat the series of three for seven times; but to be strict with ourselves and see that we only do it seven times, not once more nor once less. Then we should wait a little and try it again,—and so keep on for a number of times, repeating the same series; and we should always be sure to have the air in our bedrooms as fresh as possible. If the breathing is steady and rhythmical it helps very much, and to inhale and exhale over and over for half an hour has a very pleasant, quieting effect—sometimes such exercises make us nervous at first, and, if we are very tired, that often happens; but, if we keep steadily at work, the nervousness disappears and restful quiet follows which very often brings restoring and refreshing sleep.

Another thing to remember—and it is very important—is that an overtired brain needs more than the usual nourishment. If you have been awake for an hour, and it is three hours after your last meal, take half a cup, or a cup of hot milk. If you are awake for another two hours take half a cup more, and so, at intervals of about two hours, so long as you are awake throughout the night. Hot milk is nourishing and a sedative. It is not inconvenient to have milk by the side of one's bed, and a little saucepan and spirit lamp, so that the milk can be heated without getting up, and the quiet simple occupation of heating it is sometimes restful in itself.

There are five things to remember to help rest an overtired brain: 1. A healthy indifference to wakefulness. 2. Concentration of the mind on simple things. 3. Relaxation of the body. 4. Gentle rhythmic breathing of fresh air. 5. Regular nourishment. If we do not lose courage, but keep on steadily night after night, with a healthy persistence in remembering and practising these five things, we shall often find that what might have been a very long period of sleeplessness may be materially shortened and that the sleep which follows the practice of the exercises is better, sounder, and more refreshing, than the sleep that came before. In many cases a long or short period of insomnia can be absolutely prevented by just these simple means.

Here is perhaps the place to say that all narcotics are in such cases, absolutely pernicious.

They may bring sleep at the time, but eventually they lose their effect, and leave the nervous system in a state of strain which cannot be helped by anything but time, through much suffering that might have been avoided.

When we are not necessarily overtired but perhaps only a little tired from the day's work, it is not uncommon to be kept awake by a flapping curtain or a swinging door, by unusual noises in the streets, or by people talking. How often we hear it said, "It did seem hard when I went to bed tired last night that I should have been kept awake by a noise like that—and now this morning, I am more tired than when I went to bed."

The head nurse in a large hospital said once in distress: "I wish the nurses could be taught to step lightly over my head, so that they would not keep me awake at night." It would have been a surprise to her if she had been told that her head could be taught to yield to the steps of the nurses, so that their walking would not keep her awake.

It is resistance that keeps us awake in all such cases. The curtain flaps, and we resist it; the door swings to over and over again, and we resist it, and keep ourselves awake by wondering why it does not stop; we hear noises in the street that we am unused to, especially if we are accustomed to sleeping in the stillness of the country, and we toss and turn and wish we were in a quiet place. All the trouble comes from our own resistance to the noise, and resistance is nothing but unwillingness to submit to our conditions.

If we are willing that the curtain should go on flapping, the door go on slamming, or the noise in the street continue steadily on, our brains yield to the conditions and so sleep naturally, because the noise goes through us, so to speak, and does not run hard against our unwillingness to hear it.

There are three facts which may help to remove the resistance which naturally arises at any unusual sound when we are tired and want to get rest.

One is that in almost every sound there is a certain rhythm. If we yield to the sound enough to become sensitive to its rhythm, that, in itself, is soothing, and what before was keeping us awake now *helps us to go to sleep*. This pleasant effect of finding the rhythm in sound is especially helpful if one is inclined to lie awake while travelling in sleeping cars. The rhythm of sound and motion in sleeping cars and steamers is, in itself, soothing. If you have the habit of feeling as if you could never get refreshing sleep in a sleeping car, first be sure that you have as much fresh air as possible, and then make up your mind that you will spend the whole night, if necessary, in noticing the rhythm of the motion and sound of the cars. If you keep your mind steadily on it, you will probably be asleep in less than an hour, and, when the car stops, you will wake only enough to settle comfortably into the sense of motion when it starts again. It is pleasant to notice the gentleness with which a good engineer starts his train at night. Of course there is a difference in engineers, and some are much more gentle in starting their engines than others, but the delicacy with which the engine is started by the most expert is delightful to feel, and gives us many a lesson on the use of gentle beginnings, with other things besides locomotive engines, and especially in our dealings with each other.

The second fact with regard to yielding, instead of resisting, in order to get to sleep is that listening alone, apart from rhythm, tends to make one sleepy, and this leads us at once to the third fact, that getting to sleep is nothing but a healthy form of concentration.

If true concentration is dropping everything that interferes with fixing our attention upon some wholesome object, it means merely bringing the brain into a normal state which induces sleep when sleep is needed. First we drop everything that interferes with the one simple subject, and then we drop that, and are unconscious.

Of course it may take some time to make ourselves willing to submit to an unusual noise if we have the habit of feeling that we must necessarily be disturbed by it, and, if we can stop the noise, it is better to stop it than to give ourselves unnecessary tasks in non-resistance.

Then again, if we are overtired, our brains are sometimes so sensitive that the effect of any noise is like that of being struck in a sore spot, and then it is much more difficult to bear it, and we can only make the suffering a little less by yielding and being willing that it should go on. I cannot go to sleep while some one is knocking my lame arm, nor can I go to sleep while a noise is hitting my tired brain; but in such cases we can give up expecting to go to sleep, and get a great deal of rest by using our wills steadily not to resist; and sometimes, even then, sleep will come upon us unexpectedly.

With regard to the use of the will, perhaps the most dangerous pitfall to be avoided is the use of drugs. It is not too much to say that they never should be used at all for cases of pure sleeplessness, for with time their power to bring sleep gradually becomes exhausted, and then the patient finds himself worse off than before, for the reactionary effect of the drugs leaves him with exhausted nerves and a weakened will. All the strengthening, moral effect which can be gained from overcoming sleeplessness in wholesome ways is lost by a recourse to drugs, and character is weakened instead of strengthened.

When one has been in the habit of sleeping in the city, where the noise of the street is incessant, a change to the perfect silence of the country will often keep sleep off quite as persistently as noise. So with a man who has been in the habit of sleeping under other abnormal conditions, the change to normal conditions will sometimes keep him awake until he has adjusted himself to them, and it is not uncommon for people to be so abnormal that they resist rhythm itself, such as is heard in the rolling of the sea, or the rushing of a river.

The re-adjustment from abnormal to normal conditions of sleeping may be made surely if we set about it with a will, for we have all nature on our side. Silence is orderly for the night's rest, and rhythm only emphasizes and enhances the silence, when it is the rhythm of nature.

The habit of resistance cannot be changed in a single day—it must take time; but if the meaning, the help, and the normal power of non-resistance is clearly understood, and the effort to gain it is persistent, not only the power to sleep, but a new sense of freedom may be acquired which is quite beyond the conception of those who are in the daily habit of resistance.

When we lie down at night and become conscious that our arms and our legs and our whole bodies are resting heavily upon the bed, we are letting go all the resistance which has been left stored in our muscles from the activities of the day.

A cat, when she lies down, lets go all resistance at once, because she moves with the least possible effort; but there are very few men who do that, and so men go to their rest with more or less resistance stored in their bodies, and they must go through a conscious process of dropping it before they can settle to sleep as a normal child does, without having to think about how it is done. The conscious process, however, brings a quiet, conscious joy in the rest, which opens the mind to soothing influences, and brings a more profound refreshment than is given even to the child—and with the refreshment new power for work.

One word more about outside disturbances before we turn to those interior ones which are by far the most common preventatives of refreshing sleep. The reader will say: "How can I be willing that the noise should go on when I am not willing?" The answer is, "If you can see clearly that if you were willing, the noises would not interfere with your sleep, then you can find the ability within you to make yourself willing."

It is wonderful to realize the power we gain by compelling and controlling our desires or aversions through the intelligent use of the will, and it is easier to compel ourselves to do right against temptation than to force ourselves to do wrong against a true conviction. Indeed it is most difficult, if not impossible, to force ourselves to do wrong against a strong sense of right. Behind an our desires, aversions, and inclinations each one of us possesses a capacity for a higher will, the exercise of which, on the side of order and righteousness, brings into being the greatest power in human life. The power of character is always in harmony with the laws of truth and order, and although we must sometimes make a great effort of the will to do right against our inclinations the ease of such effort increases as the power of character increases, and strength of will grows steadily by use, because it receives its life from the eternal will and is finding its way to harmony with that.

It is the lower, selfish will that often keeps us awake by causing interior disturbances.

An actor may have a difficult part to play, and feel that a great deal depends upon his success. He stays awake with anxiety, and this anxiety is nothing but resistance to the possibility of failure. The first thing for him to do is to teach himself to be willing to fail. If he becomes willing to fail, then all his anxiety will go, and he will be able to sleep and get the rest and new life which he needs in order to play the part well. If he is willing to fail, then all the nervous force which before was being wasted in anxiety is set free for use in the exercise of his art.

Looking forward to what is going to happen on the next day, or within a few days, may cause so much anxiety as to keep us awake; but if we have a good, clear sense of the futility of resistance, whether our expected success or failure depends on ourselves or on others, we can compel ourselves to a quiet willingness which will make our brains quiet and receptive to restful sleep, and so enable us to wake with new power for whatever task or pleasure may lie before us.

Of course we are often kept awake by the sense of having done wrong. In such cases the first thing to do is to make a free acknowledgment to ourselves of the wrong we have done, and then to make up our minds to do the right thing at once. That, if the wrong done is not too serious, will put us to sleep; and if the next day we go about our work remembering the lesson we have learned, we probably will have little trouble in sleeping.

If Macbeth had had the truth and courage to tell Lady Macbeth that both he and she were wicked plotters and murderers, and that he intended, for his part, to stop being a scoundrel, and, if he had persisted in carrying out his good intentions, he would never have "murdered sleep."

III.
Resistance

A MAN once grasped a very hot poker with his hand, and although he cried out with pain, held on to the poker. His friend called out to him to drop it, whereupon the man indignantly cried out the more.

"Drop it? How can you expect me to think of dropping it with pain like this? I tell you when a man is suffering, as I am, he can think of nothing but the pain."

And the more indignant he was, the tighter he held on to the poker, and the more he cried out with pain.

This story in itself is ridiculous, but it is startlingly true as an illustration of what people are doing every day.

There is an instinct in us to drop every hot poker at once; and probably we should be able to drop any other form of unnecessary disagreeable sensation as soon as possible, if we had not lost that wholesome instinct through want of use. As it is, we must learn to re-acquire the lost faculty by the deliberate use of our intelligence and will.

It is as if we had lost our freedom and needed to be shown the way back to it, step by step. The process is slow but very interesting, if we are in earnest; and when, after wandering in the bypaths, we finally strike the true road, we find our lost faculty waiting for us, and all that we have learned in reaching it is so much added power.

But at present we are dealing in the main with a world which has no suspicion of such instincts or faculties as these, and is suffering along in blind helplessness. A man will drop a hot poker as soon as he feels it burn, but he will tighten his muscles and hold on to a cold in his head so persistently that he only gets rid of it at all because nature is stronger than he is, and carries it off in spite of him.

How common it is to see a woman entirely wrapped up, with a handkerchief held to her nose,—the whole body as tense as it can be,—wondering "Why does it take so long to get rid of this cold?" To get free from a severe cold there should be open and clear circulation throughout the whole body. The more the circulation is impeded, the longer the cold will last. To begin with, the cold itself impedes the circulation; and if, in addition, we offer resistance to the very idea of having a cold, we tighten our nerves and our bodies and thereby impede our circulation still further.

It is curious that the more we resist a cold the more we hold on to it, but it is a very evident fact; and so is its logical corollary, that the less we resist it the sooner it leaves us.

It would seem absurd to people who do not understand, to say:—

"I have caught cold, I must relax and let it go through me."

But the literal truth is that when we relax, we open the channels of circulation in our bodies, and so allow the cold to be carried off. In addition to the relaxing, long, quiet breaths help the circulation still more, and so help the cold to go off sooner.

In the same way people resist pain and hold on to it; when they are attacked with severe pain, they at once devote their entire attention to the sensation of pain, instead of devoting it to the best means of getting relief. They double themselves up tight, and hold on to the place that hurts. Then all the nervous force tends toward the sore place and the tension retards the circulation and makes it difficult for nature to cure the pain, as she would spontaneously if she were only allowed to have her own way.

I once knew a little girl who, whenever she hit one elbow, would at once deliberately rub the other. She said that she had discovered that it took her mind away from the elbow that hurt, and so stopped its hurting sooner. The use of a counterirritant is not uncommon with good physicians, but the counter-irritant only does what is much more effectually accomplished when the patient uses his will and intelligence to remove the original irritant by ceasing to resist it.

A man who was troubled with spasmodic contraction of the throat once went to a doctor in alarm and distress. The doctor told him that, in any case, nothing worse than fainting could happen to him, and that, if he fainted away, his throat would be relieved, because the fainting would relax the muscles of the throat, and the only trouble with it was contraction. Singularly, it did not seem to occur to the doctor that the man might be taught to relax his throat by the use of his own will, instead of having to faint away in order that nature might do it for him. Nature would be just as ready to help us if we were intelligent, as when she has to knock us down, in order that she may do for us what we do not know enough to do for ourselves.

There is no illness that could not be much helped by quiet relaxing on the part of the patient, so as to allow nature and remedial agencies to do their work more easily.

That which keeps relief away in the case of the cold, of pain, and of many illnesses, is the contraction of the nerves and muscles of the body, which impedes the curative power of its healing forces. The contraction of the nerves and muscles of the body is caused by resistance in the mind, and resistance in the mind is unwillingness: unwillingness to endure the distress of the cold, the pain, or the illness, whatever it may be; and the more unwilling we are to suffer from illness, the more we are hindering nature from bringing about a cure.

One of the greatest difficulties in life is illness when the hands are full of work, and of business requiring attention. In many eases the strain and anxiety, which causes resistance to the illness, is even more severe, and makes more trouble than the illness itself.

Suppose, for instance, that a man is taken down with the measles, when he feels that he ought to be at his office, and that his absence may result in serious loss to himself and others. If he begins by letting go, in his body and in his mind, and realizing that the illness is beyond his own power, it will soon occur to him that he might as well turn his illness to account by getting a good rest out of it. In this frame of mind his chances of early recovery will be increased, and he may even get up from his illness with so much new life and with his mind so much refreshed as to make up, in part, for his temporary absence from business. But, on the other hand, if he resists, worries, complains and gets irritable, he irritates his nervous system and, by so doing is likely to bring on any one of the disagreeable troubles that are known to follow measles; and thus he may keep himself housed for weeks, perhaps months, instead of days.

Another advantage in dropping all resistance to illness, is that the relaxation encourages a restful attitude of mind, which enables us to take the right amount of time for recovery, and so prevents either a possible relapse, or our feeling only half well for a long time, when we might have felt wholly well from the time we first began to take up our life again. Indeed the advantages of nonresistance in such cases are innumerable, and there are no advantages whatever in resistance and unwillingness.

Clear as these things must be to any intelligent person whose attention is turned in the right direction, it seems most singular that not in one case in a thousand are they deliberately practised. People seem to have lost their common sense with regard to them, because for generations the desire for having our own way has held us in bondage, and confused our standard of freedom; more than that, it has befogged our sense of natural law, and the result is that we painfully fight to make water run up hill when, if we were to give one quiet look, we should see that better things could be accomplished, and our own sense of freedom become keener, by being content to let the water quietly run down and find its own level.

It is not normal to be ill and to be kept from our everyday use, but it is still less normal for a healthy, intelligent mind to keep its body ill longer than is necessary by resisting the fact of illness. Every disease, though it is abnormal in itself, may frequently be kept within bounds by a certain normal course of conduct, and, if our suffering from the disease itself is unavoidable, by far our wisest course is to stand aside, so to speak, and let it take its own course, using all necessary remedies and precautions in order that the attack may be as mild as possible.

Many readers, although they see the common sense of such non-resistance, will find it difficult to practise it, because of their inheritances and personal habits.

The man who held the hot poker only needed to drop it with his fingers; the man who is taken ill only needs to be willing with his mind and to relax with his nerves in order to hasten his recovery.

A very useful practice is to talk to ourselves so quietly and earnestly as to convince our brains of the true helpfulness of being willing and of the impediment of our unwillingness. Tell the truth to yourself over and over, quietly and without emotion, and steadily and firmly contradict every temptation to think that it is impossible not to resist. If men could once be convinced of the very real and wonderful power they have of teaching their own brains, and exacting obedience from them, the resulting new life and ability for use would make the world much happier and stronger.

This power of separating the clear, quiet common sense in ourselves from the turbulent, willful rebellion and resistance, and so quieting our selfish natures and compelling them to normal behavior, is truly latent in us all. It may be difficult at first to use it, especially in cases of strong, perverted natures and fixed habits, because in such cases our resistances are harder and more interior, but if we keep steadily on, aiming in the right direction,—if we persist in the practice of keeping ourselves separate from our unproductive turbulences, and of teaching our brains what we *know* to be the truth, we shall finally find ourselves walking on level ground, instead of climbing painfully up hill. Then we shall be only grateful for all the hard work which was the means of bringing us into the clear air of freedom.

There could not be a better opportunity to begin our training in non-resistance than that which illness affords.

IV.
Hurry, Worry, and Irritability

PROBABLY most people have had the experience of hurrying to a train with the feeling that something held them back, but not many have observed that their muscles, under such conditions, actually *do* pull them back.

If any one wants to prove the correctness of this observation let him watch himself, especially if it is necessary for him to go downstairs to get to the station, while he is walking down the steps. The drawing back or contracting of the muscles, as if they were intelligently trying to prevent us from reaching the train on time, is most remarkable. Of course all that impeding contraction comes from resistance, and it seems at first sight very strange that we should resist the accomplishment of the very thing we want to do. Why should I resist the idea of catching a train, when at the same time I am most anxious to do so? Why should my muscles reflect that resistance by contracting, so that they directly impede my progress? It seems a most singular case of a house divided against itself for me to want to take a train, and for my own muscles, which are given me for my command, to refuse to take me there, so that I move toward the train with an involuntary effort away from it. But when the truth is recognized, all this muscular contraction is easily explained. What we are resisting is not the fact of taking the train, but the possibility of losing it. That resistance reflects itself upon our muscles and causes them to contract. Although this is a practical truth, it takes us some time to realize that the fear of losing the train is often the only thing that prevents our catching it. If we could once learn this fact thoroughly, and live from our clearer knowledge, it would be one of the greatest helps toward taking all things in life quietly and without necessary strain. For the fact holds good in all hurry. It is the fear of not accomplishing what is before us in time that holds us back from its accomplishment.

This is so helpful and so useful a truth that I feel it necessary to repeat it in many ways. Fear brings resistance, resistance impedes our progress. Our faculties are paralyzed by lack of confidence, and confidence is the result of a true consciousness of our powers when in harmony with law. Often the fear of not accomplishing what is before us is the *only* thing that stands in our way.

If we put all hurry, whether it be an immediate hurry to catch a train, or the hurry of years toward the accomplishment of the main objects of our lives,—if we put it all under the clear light of this truth, it will eventually relieve us of a strain which is robbing our vitality to no end.

First, the times that we *must* hurry should be minimized. In nine cases out of ten the necessity for hurry comes only from our own attitude of mind, and from no real need whatever. In the tenth case we must learn to hurry with our muscles, and not with our nerves, or, I might better say, we must hurry without excitement. To hurry quietly is to most people an unknown thing, but when hurry is a necessity, the process of successive effort in it should be pleasant and refreshing.

If in the act of needful hurry we are constantly teaching ourselves to stop resistance by saying over and over, through whatever we may be doing, "I am perfectly willing to lose that train, I am willing to lose it, I am willing to lose it," that will help to remove the resistance, and so help us to learn how to make haste quietly.

But the reader will say, "How can I make myself willing when I am not willing?"

The answer is that if you know that your unwillingness to lose the train is preventing you from catching it, you certainly will see the efficacy of being willing, and you will do all in your power toward yielding to common sense. Unwillingness is resistance,—resistance in the mind contracts the muscles, and such contraction prevents our using the muscles freely and easily. Therefore let us be willing.

Of course there is a lazy, selfish indifference to catching a train, or accomplishing anything else, which leaves the tendency to hurry out of some temperaments altogether, but with that kind of a person we are not dealing now. And such indifference is the absolute opposite of the wholesome indifference in which there is no touch of laziness or selfishness.

If we want to avoid hurry we must get the habit of hurry out of our brains, and cut ourselves off, patiently and kindly, from the atmosphere of hurry about us. The habit gets so strong a hold of the nerves, and is impressed upon them so forcibly as a steady tendency, that it can be detected by a close observer even in a person who is lying on a lounge in the full belief that he is resting. It shows itself especially in the breathing. A wise athlete has said that our normal breathing should consist of six breaths to one minute. If the reader will try this rate of breathing, the slowness of it will surprise him. Six breaths to one minute seem to make the breathing unnecessarily slow, and just double that seems about the right number for ordinary people; and the habit of breathing at this slower rate is a great help, from a physical standpoint, toward erasing the tendency to hurry.

One of the most restful exercises any one can take is to lie at full length on a bed or lounge and to inhale and exhale, at a perfectly even, slow rate, for half an hour. It makes the exercise more restful if another person counts for the breathing, say, ten slowly and quickly to inhale, and ten to exhale, with a little pause to give time for a quiet change from one breath to another.

Resistance, which is the mental source of hurry, is equally at the root of that most harmful emotion—the habit of worrying. And the same truths which must be learned and practised to free ourselves of the one habit are applicable to the other.

Take the simple example of a child who worries over his lessons. Children illustrate the principle especially well, because they are so responsive that, if you meet them quietly with the truth in difficulties of this kind they recognize its value and apply it very quickly, and it takes them, comparatively, a very little time to get free.

If you think of telling a child that the moment he finds himself worrying about his lesson he should close his book and say:

"I do not care whether I get this lesson or not."

And then, when he has actually persuaded himself that he does not care, that he should open his book and study,—it would seem, at first sight, that he would find it difficult to understand you; but, on the contrary, a child understands more quickly than older people, for the child has not had time to establish himself so firmly in the evil habit.

I have in mind a little girl in whom the habit had begun of worrying lest she should fail in her lessons, especially in her Latin. Her mother sent her to be taught how not to worry. The teacher, after giving her some idea of the common sense of not worrying, taught her quieting exercises which she practised every day; and when one day, in the midst of one of her lessons, Margaret seemed very quiet and restful, the teacher asked:—

"Margaret, could you worry about your Latin now if you tried?"

"Yes," said Margaret, "I am afraid I could."

Nothing more was said, but she went on with her lessons, and several days after, during the same restful quiet time, the teacher ventured again.

"Now, Margaret, could you worry about your Latin if you tried?"

Then came the emphatic answer, *"No, I could not."*

After that the little girl would say:

"With the part of me that worries, I do not care whether I get my Latin or not; with the part of me that does not worry, I want to get my Latin very much; therefore I will stay in the part of me that does not worry, and get my Latin."

A childish argument, and one that may be entirely incomprehensible to many minds, but to those who do comprehend, it represents a very real and practical help.

It is, in most cases, a grave mistake to, reason with a worry. We must first drop the worry, and then do our reasoning. If to drop the worry seems impossible, we can separate ourselves from it enough to prevent it from interfering with our reasoning, very much as if it were neuralgia. There is never any real reason for a worry, because, as we all know, worry never helps us to gain, and often is the cause of our losing, the things which we so much desire.

Sometimes we worry because we are tired, and in that case, if we can recognize the real cause, we should use our wills to withdraw our attention from the object of worry, and to get all possible rest at once, in the confident belief that rest will make things clear, or at least more clear than they were when we were tired. It would be hard to compute the harm that has been done by kindly disposed people in reasoning with the worry of a friend, when the anxiety is increased by fatigue or illness. To reason with one who is tired or ill and worried, only increases the mental strain, and every effort that is made to reason him out of it aggravates the strain; until, finally, the poor brain, through kindly meant effort, has been worked into an extreme state of irritation or even inflammation. For the same reason, a worried mind should not be laughed at. Worries that are aroused by fatigue or illness are often most absurd, but they are not absurd to the mind that is suffering from them, and to make fun of them only brings more pain, and more worry. Gentle, loving attention, with kindly, truthful answers, will always help. By such attention we are really giving no importance to the worry, but only to our friend, with the hope of soothing and quieting him out of his worries, and when he is rested he may see the truth for himself.

We should deal with ourselves, in such cases, as gently as we would with a friend, excepting that we can tell the truth to ourselves more plainly than we can to most friends.

Worrying is resistance, resistance is unwillingness. Unwillingness interferes with whatever we may want to accomplish. To be willing that this, that, or the other should happen seems most difficult, when to our minds, this, that, or the other would bring disaster. And yet if we can once see clearly that worrying resistance tends toward disaster rather than away from it, or, at the very least, takes away our strength and endurance, it is only a matter of time before we become able to drop our resistance altogether. But it is a matter of time; and, when once we are faced toward freedom, we must be patient and steady, and not expect to gain very rapidly. Theirs is indeed a hard lot who have acquired this habit of worry, and persist in doing nothing to gain their freedom.

"Now I have got something to worry about for the rest of my life," remarked a poor woman once. Her face was set toward worrying; nothing but her own will could have turned it the other way, and yet she deliberately chose not to use it, and so she was fixed and settled in prison for the rest of her life.

To worry is wicked; it is wickedness of a kind that people often do not recognize as such, and they are not fully responsible until they do; but to prove it to be wicked is an easy matter, when once we are faced toward freedom; and, to get over it, as I have said, is a matter of steady, persistent patience.

As for irritability, that is also resistance; but there are two kinds of irritability,—physical and moral.

There is an irritability that comes when we are hungry, if we have eaten something that disagrees with us, if we are cold or tired or uncomfortable from some other physical cause. When we feel that kind of irritability we should ignore it, as we would ignore a little snapping dog across the street, while at the same time removing its cause as quickly as we can. There is nothing that delights the devil more than to scratch a man with the irritability of hunger, and have him respond to it at once by being ugly and rude to a friend; for then the irritation immediately becomes moral, and every bit of selfishness rushes up to join it, and to arouse whatever there may be of evil in the man. It is simple to recognize this merely physical form of irritability, and we should no more allow ourselves to speak, or act, or even *think* from it, than we should allow ourselves to walk directly into foul air, when the good fresh air is close to us on the other side.

But moral irritability is more serious; that comes from the soul, and is the result of our wanting our own way. The immediate cause may be some physical disturbance, such as noise, or it may be aroused by other petty annoyances, like that of being obliged to wait for some one who is unpunctual, or by disagreement in an argument. There are very many causes for irritability, and we each have our own individual sensitiveness or antipathy, but, whatever the secondary cause, the primary cause is always the same,—resistance or unwillingness to accept our circumstances.

If we are fully willing to be disturbed, we cease to be troubled by the disturbance; if we are willing to wait, we are not annoyed by being kept waiting, and we are in a better, more quiet humor to help our friend to the habit of promptness. If we are willing that another should differ from us in opinion, we can see more clearly either to convince our friend, if he is wrong,—or to admit that he is right, and that we are wrong. The essential condition of good argument is freedom from personal feeling, with the desire only for the truth,—whether it comes from one party or the other.

Hurry, worry, and irritability all come from selfish resistance to the facts of life, and the only permanent cure for the waste of force and the exhausting distress which they entail, is a willingness to accept those facts, whatever they may be, in a spirit of cheerful and reverent obedience to law.

V.
Nervous Fears

TO argue with nervous anxiety, either in ourselves or in others, is never helpful. Indeed it is never helpful to argue with "nerves" at all. Arguing with nervous excitement of any kind is like rubbing a sore. It only irritates it. It does not take long to argue excited or tired nerves into inflammation, but it is a long and difficult process to allay the inflammation when it has once been aroused. It is a sad fact that many people have been argued into long nervous illnesses by would-be kind friends whose only intention was to argue them out of illness. Even the kindest and most disinterested friends are apt to lose patience when they argue, and that, to the tired brain which they are trying to relieve, is a greater irritant than they realize. The radical cure for nervous fears is to drop resistance to painful circumstances or conditions. Resistance is unwillingness to endure, and to drop the resistance is to be strongly willing. This vigorous "willingness" is so absolutely certain in its happy effect, and is so impossible that it should fail, that the resistant impulses seem to oppose themselves to it with extreme energy. It is as if the resistances were conscious imps, and as if their certainty of defeat—in the case of their victim's entire "willingness "—roused them to do their worst, and to hold on to their only possible means of power with all the more determination. Indeed, when a man is working through a hard state, in gaining his freedom from nervous fears, these imps seem to hold councils of war, and to devise new plans of attack in order to take him by surprise and overwhelm him in an emergency. But every sharp attack, if met with quiet "willingness," brings a defeat for the assailants, until finally the resistant imps are conquered and disappear. Occasionally a stray imp will return, and try to arouse resistance on what he feels is old familiar ground, but he is quickly driven off, and the experience only makes a man more quietly vigilant and more persistently "willing."

Perhaps one of the most prevalent and one of the hardest fears to meet, is that of insanity,—especially when it is known to be a probable or possible inheritance. When such fear is oppressing a man,—to tell him that he not only can get free from the fear, but free from any possibility of insanity, through a perfect willingness to be insane, must seem to him at first a monstrous mockery; and, if you cannot persuade him of the truth, but find that you are only frightening him more, there is nothing to do then but to be willing that he should not be persuaded, and to wait for a better opportunity. You can show him that no such inheritance can become an actuality, unless we permit it, and that the very knowledge of an hereditary tendency, when wholesomely used, makes it possible for us to take every precaution and to use every true safeguard against it. The presence of danger is a source of strength to the brave; and the source of abiding courage is not in the nerves, but in the spirit and the will behind them. It is the clear statement of this fact that will persuade him The fact may have to be stated many times, but it should never be argued. And the more quietly and gently and earnestly it is stated, the sooner it will convince, for it is the truth that makes us free.

Fear keeps the brain in a state of excitement. Even when it is not consciously felt, it is felt sub-consciously, and we ought to be glad to have it aroused, in order that we may see it and free ourselves, not only from the particular fear for the time being, but from the subconscious impression of fear in general.

Is seems curious to speak of grappling with the fear of insanity, and conquering it by being perfectly willing to be insane, but it is no more curious than the relation of the centrifugal and the centripetal forces to each other. We need our utmost power of concentration to enable us to yield truly, and to be fully willing to submit to whatever the law of our being may require. Fear contracts the brain and the nerves, and interrupts the circulation, and want of free circulation is a breeder of disease. Dropping resistance relaxes the tension of the brain and nerves, and opens the channels for free circulation, and free circulation helps to carry off the tendency to disease. If a man is wholesomely willing to be insane, should such an affliction overtake him, he has dropped all resistance to the idea of insanity, and thus also to all the mental and physical contractions that would foster insanity. He has dropped a strain which was draining his brain of its proper strength, and the result is new vigor to mind and body. To drop an inherited strain produces a great and wonderful change, and all we need to bring it about is to thoroughly understand how possible and how beneficial it is. If we once realize the benefit of dropping the strain, our will is there to accomplish the rest, as surely as it is there to take our hand out of the fire when it burns.

Then there is the fear of contagion. Some people are haunted with the fear of catching disease, and the contraction which such resistance brings induces a physical state most favorable to contagion. There was once a little child whose parents were so full of anxious fears that they attempted to protect him from disease in ways that were extreme and ridiculous. All his toys were boiled, everything he ate or drank was sterilized, and many other precautions were taken,—but along with all the precautions, the parents were in constant fear; and it is not unreasonable to feel that the reflection upon the child of the chronic resistance to possible danger with which he was surrounded, had something to do with the fact that the dreaded disease was finally caught, and that, moreover, the child did not recover. If reasonably healthy conditions had been insisted upon, and the parents had felt a wholesome trust in the general order of things, it would have been likely to make the child more vigorous, and would have tended to increase his capacity for throwing off contagion.

Children are very sensitive, and it is not unusual to see a child crying because its mother is out of humor, even though she may not have spoken a cross word. It is not unusual to see a child contract its little brain and body in response to the fears and contractions of its parents, and such contraction keeps the child in a state in which it may be more difficult to throw off disease.

If you hold your fist as tight as you can hold it for fifteen minutes, the fatigue you will feel when it relaxes is a clear proof of the energy you have been wasting. The waste of nervous energy would be much increased if the fist were held tightly for hours; and if the waste is so great in the useless tightening of a fist, it is still greater in the extended and continuous contraction of brain and nerves in useless fears; and the energy saved through dropping the fears and their accompanying tension can bring in the same proportion a vigor unknown before, and at the same time afford protection against the very things we feared.

The fear of taking cold is so strong in many people that a draught of fresh air becomes a bugaboo to their contracted, sensitive nerves. Draughts are imagined as existing everywhere, and the contraction which immediately follows the sensation of a draught is the best means of preparing to catch a cold.

Fear of accident keeps one in a constant state of unnecessary terror. To be willing that an accident should happen does not make it more likely to happen, but it prevents our wasting energy by resistance, and keeps us quiet and free, so that if an emergency of any kind arises, we are prepared to act promptly and calmly for the best. If the amount of human energy wasted in the strain of nervous fear could be measured in pounds of pressure, the figures would be astonishing. Many people who have the habit of nervous fear in one form or another do not throw it off merely because they do not know how. There are big and little nervous fears, and each and all can be met and conquered,—thus bringing a freedom of life which cannot even be imagined by those carrying the burden of fear, more or less, throughout their lives.

The fear of what people will think of us is a very common cause of slavery, and the nervous anxiety as to whether we do or do not please is a strain which wastes the energy of the greater part of mankind. It seems curious to measure the force wasted in sensitiveness to public opinion as you would measure the waste of power in an engine, and yet it is a wholesome and impersonal way to think of it,—until we find a better way. It relieves us of the morbid element in the sensitiveness to say, "I cannot mind what so-and-so thinks of me, for I have not the nervous energy to spare." It relieves us still more of the tendency to morbid feeling, if we are wholesomely interested in what others think of us, in order to profit by it, and do better. There is nothing morbid or nervous about our sensitiveness to opinion, when it is derived from a love of criticism for the sake of its usefulness. Such a rightful and wise regard for the opinion of others results in a saving of energy, for on the one hand, it saves us from the mistakes of false and shallow independence, and, on the other, from the wasteful strain of servile fear.

The little nervous fears are countless. The fear of not being exact. The fear of not having turned off the gas entirely. The fear of not having done a little daily duty which we find again and again we have done. These fears are often increased, and sometimes are aroused, by our being tired, and it is well to realize that, and to attend at once carefully to whatever our particular duty may be, and then, when the fear of not having done it attacks us, we should think of it as if it were a physical pain, and turn our attention quietly to something else. In this way such little nagging fears are relieved; whereas, if we allowed ourselves to be driven by them, we might bring on nervous states that would take weeks or months to overcome. These nervous fears attack us again and again in subtle ways, if we allow ourselves to be influenced by them. They are all forms of unwillingness or resistance, and may all be removed by dropping the resistance and yielding,—not to the fear, but to a willingness that the fear should be there.

One of the small fears that often makes life seem unbearable is the fear of a dentist. A woman who had suffered from this fear for a lifetime, and who had been learning to drop resistances in other ways, was once brought face to face with the necessity for going to the dentist, and the old fear was at once aroused,—something like the feeling one might have in preparing for the guillotine,—and she suffered from it a day or two before she remembered her new principles. Then, when the new ideas came back to her mind, she at once applied them and said, "Yes, I *am afraid,* I *am awfully afraid.* I am *perfectly willing to be afraid,"* and the ease with which the fear disappeared was a surprise,—even to herself.

Another woman who was suffering intensely from fear as to the after-effects of an operation, had begun to tremble with great nervous intensity. The trembling itself frightened her, and when a friend told her quietly to be willing to tremble, her quick, intelligence responded at once. "Yes," she said, "I will, I will make myself tremble," and, by not only being willing to tremble, but by making herself tremble, she got quiet mental relief in a very short time, and the trembling disappeared.

The fear of death is, with its derivatives, of course, the greatest of all; and to remove our resistance to the idea of death, by being perfectly willingly to die is to remove the foundation of all the physical cowardice in life, and to open the way for the growth of a courage which is strength and freedom itself. He who yields gladly to the ordinary facts of life, will also yield gladly to the supreme fact of physical death, for a brave and happy willingness is the characteristic habit of his heart:—

> Under the wide and starry sky,
> Dig the grave and let me lie.
> Glad did I live and gladly die,
> And I laid me down with a will."

There is a legend of the Arabs in which a man puts his head out of his tent and says, "I will loose my camel and commit him to God," and a neighbor who hears him says, in his turn, "I will tie my camel and commit him to God." The true helpfulness from non-resistance does not come from neglecting to take proper precautions against the objects of fear, but from yielding with entire willingness to the necessary facts of life, and a sane confidence that, whatever comes, we shall be provided with the means of meeting it. This confidence is, in itself, one of the greatest sources of intelligent endurance.

VI.
Self-Consciousness

SELF-CONSCIOUSNESS may be truly defined as a person's inability to get out of his own way. There are, however, some people who are so entirely and absolutely self-conscious that everything they do, even though it may appear spontaneous and ingenuous, is observed and admired and approved of by themselves,—indeed they are supported and sustained by their self-consciousness. They are so completely in bondage to themselves that they have no glimpse of the possibility of freedom, and therefore this bondage is pleasant to them.

With these people we have, at present, nothing to do; it is only those who have begun to realize their bondage as such, or who suffer from it, that can take any steps toward freedom. The self-satisfied slaves must stay in prison until they see where they are—and it is curious and sad to see them rejoicing in bondage and miscalling it freedom. It makes one long to see them struck by an emergency, bringing a flash of inner light which is often the beginning of an entire change of state. Sometimes the enlightenment comes through one kind of circumstance, sometimes through another; but, if the glimpse of clearer sight it brings is taken advantage of, it will be followed by a time of groping in the dark, and always by more or less suffering. When, however, we know that we are in the dark, there is hope of our coming to the light; and suffering is nothing whatever after it is over and has brought its good results.

If we were to take away the prop of self-approval entirely and immediately from any one of the habitually self-satisfied people, the probable result would be an entire nervous collapse, or even a painful form of insanity; and, in all changes of state from bondage to freedom, the process is and must be exceedingly slow. No one ever strengthened his character with a wrench of impatience, although we are often given the opportunity for a firm and immediate use of the will which leaves lasting strength behind it. For the main growth of our lives, however, we must be steadily patient, content to aim in the true direction day by day, hour by hour, minute by minute. If we fall, we must pick ourselves up and go right on,—not stop to be discouraged for one instant after we have recognized our state as a temptation. Whatever the stone may be that we have tripped over, we have learned that it is there, and, while we may trip over the same stone many times, if we learn our lesson each time, it decreases the possible number of stumbles, and smooths our paths more than we know.

There is no exception to the necessity for this patient, steady plodding in the work required to gain our freedom from self-consciousness. It is when we are aware of our bondage that our opportunity to gain our freedom from it really begins. This bondage brings very real suffering, and we may often, without exaggeration, call it torture. It is sometimes even extreme torture, but may have to be endured for a lifetime unless the sufferer has the clear light by which to find his freedom; and, unfortunately, many who might have the light will not use it because they are unwilling to recognize the selfishness that is at the root of their trouble. Some women like to call it "shyness," because the name sounds well, and seems to exonerate them from any responsibility with regard to their defect. Men will rarely speak of their self-consciousness, but, when they do, they are apt to speak of it with more or less indignation and self-pity, as if they were in the clutches of something extraneous to themselves, and over which they can never gain control. If, when a man is complaining of self-consciousness and of its interference with his work in life, you tell him in all kindness that all his suffering has its root in downright selfishness, he will, in most cases, appear not to hear, or he will beg the question, and, having avoided acknowledging the truth, will continue to complain and ask for help, and perhaps wonder whether hypnotism may not help him, or some other form of "cure." Anything rather than look the truth in the face and do the work in himself which, is the only possible road to lasting, freedom. Self-pity, and what may be called spiritual laziness, is at the root of most of the self-torment in the world.

How ridiculous it would seem if a man tried to produce an electric burner according to laws of his own devising, and then sat down and pitied himself because the light would not burn, instead of searching about until he had found the true laws of electricity whose application would make the light shine successfully. How ridiculous it would seem if a man tried to make water run up hill without providing that it should do so by reaching its own level, and then got indignant because he did not succeed, and wondered if there were not some "cure" by means of which his object might be accomplished. And yet it is no more strange for a man to disobey habitually the laws of character, and then to suffer for his disobedience, and wonder why he suffers.

There is an external necessity for obeying social laws which must be respected, or society would go to pieces; and there is just as great an internal necessity for obeying spiritual laws to gain our proper self-control and power for use; but we do not recognize that necessity because, while disregarding the laws of character, we can still live without the appearance of doing harm to the community. Social laws can be respected in the letter but not in the spirit, whereas spiritual laws must be accepted by the individual heart and practiced by the individual will in order to produce any useful result. Each one of us must do the required work in himself. There is no "cure," no help from outside which can bring one to a lasting freedom.

If self-consciousness makes us blush, the more we are troubled the more it increases, until the blushing may become so unbearable that we are tempted to keep away from people altogether; and thus life, so far as human fellowship goes, would become more and more limited. But, when such a limitation is allowed to remain within us, and we make no effort of our own to find its root and to exterminate it, it warps us through and through. If self-consciousness excites us to talk, and we talk on and on to no end, simply allowing the selfish suffering to goad us, the habit weakens our brains so that in time they lose the power of strong consecutive thought and helpful brevity.

If self-consciousness causes us to wriggle, and strain, and stammer, and we do not recognize the root of the trouble and shun it, and learn to yield and quietly relax our nerves and muscles, of course the strain becomes worse. Then, rather than suffer from it any longer, we keep away from people, just as the blushing man is tempted to do. In that case, the strain is still in us, in the back of our brains, so to speak—because we have not faced and overcome it.

Stage fright is an intense form of self-consciousness, but the man who is incapable of stage fright lacks the sensitive temperament required to achieve great power as an artist. The man who overcomes stage fright by getting out of his own way, and by letting the character he is playing, or the music he is interpreting, work through him as a clear, unselfish channel receives new power for his work in the proportion that he shuns his own interfering selfishness.

But it is with the self-consciousness of everyday life that we have especially to do now, and with the practical wisdom necessary to gain freedom from all its various discomforts; and, even more than that, to gain the new power for useful service which comes from the possession of that freedom.

The remedy is to be found in obedience to the law of unselfishness, carried out into the field of nervous suffering.

Whatever one may think, however one may try to dodge the truth by this excuse or that, the conditions to be fulfilled in order to gain freedom from self-consciousness are *absolutely within the individual who suffers.* When we once understand this, and are faced toward the truth, we are sure to find our way out, with more or less rapidity, according to the strength with which we use our wills in true obedience.

First, we must be willing to accept the effects of self-consciousness. The more we resist these effects the more they force themselves upon us, and the more we suffer from them. We must be willing to blush, be willing to realize that we have talked too much, and perhaps made ourselves ridiculous. We must be willing to feel the discomforts of self-consciousness in whatever form they may appear. Then—the central point of all—we must know and understand, and not dodge in the very least the truth that the *root of self-consciousness is selfishly caring what other people think of us,—and wanting to appear well before them.*

Many readers of this article who suffer from self-consciousness will want to deny this; others will acknowledge it, but will declare their inability to live according to the truth; some,—perhaps more than a few,—will recognize the truth and set to work with a will to obey it, and how happily we may look forward to the freedom which will eventually be theirs!

A wise man has said that when people do not think well of us, the first thing to do is to look and see whether they are right. In most cases, even though they way have unkind feelings mingled with their criticism, there is an element of truth in it from which we may profit. In such cases we are much indebted to our critics, for, by taking their suggestions, we are helped toward strength of character and power for use. If there is no truth in the criticism, we need not think of it at all, but live steadily on, knowing that the truth will take care of itself.

We should be willing that any one should think *anything* of us, so long as we have the strength of a good conscience. We should be willing to appear in any light if that appearance will enhance our use, or is a necessity of growth. If an awkward appearance is necessary in the process of our journey toward freedom, we must not resist the fact of its existence, and should only dwell on it long enough to shun its cause in so far as we can, and gain the good result of the greater freedom which will follow.

It is because the suffering from self-consciousness is often so intense that freedom from it brings, by contrast, so happy and so strong a sense of power.

There is a school for the treatment of stammerers in this country in which the pupils are initiated into the process of cure by being required to keep silence for a week. This would be a most helpful beginning in a training to overcome self-consciousness. We should recognize first that we must be willing to endure the effects of self-consciousness without resistance. Secondly, we should admit that the root of self-consciousness lies entirely in a selfish desire to appear well before others. If, while recognizing these two essential truths and confirming them until they are thoroughly implanted in our brains, we should quietly persist in going among people, the practice of silent attention to others would be of the greatest value in gaining real freedom. The practice of attentive and sympathetic silence might well be followed by people in general far more than it is. The protection of a loving, unselfish silence is very great: a silence which is the result of shunning all selfish, self-assertive, vain, or affected speech; a silence which is never broken for the sake of "making conversation," "showing off," or covering selfish embarrassment; a silence which is full of sympathy and interest,—the power of such a silence cannot be overestimated.

If we have the evil habit of talking for the sake of winning approval, we should practise this silence; or if we talk for the sake of calling attention to ourselves, for the sake of winning sympathy for our selfish pains and sorrows, or for the sake of indulging in selfish emotions, nothing can help us more than the habit of loving and attentive silence.

Only when we know how to practise this—in an impersonal, free and quiet spirit, one which is not due to outward repression of any kind—are we able to talk with quiet, loving, helpful speech. Then may we tell the clean truth without giving unnecessary offence, and then may we soothe and rest, as well as stimulate in, wholesome ways; then, also, will our minds open to receive the good that may come to us through the words and actions of others.

VII.
The Circumstances of Life

IT is not the circumstances of life that trouble or weigh upon us, it is the way we take them. If a man is playing a difficult game of chess, the more intricate the moves the more thoughtfully he looks over his own and his opponent's men, and the more fully he is aroused to make the right move toward a checkmate. If, when the game became difficult, the player stopped to be depressed and disheartened, his opponent would probably always checkmate him; whereas, in most cases, the more difficult the game the more thoroughly the players are aroused to do their best, and a difficult game is invariably a good one,—the winner and the loser both feel it to be so,—even though the loser may regret his loss. But—the reader will say—a game of chess is a game only,—neither one's bread and butter nor one's life depend upon winning or losing it. If, however, we need to be cool and quiet and trustful for a game, which is merely an amusement, and if we play the game better for being cool and quiet and trustful, why is not a quiet steadiness in wrestling with the circumstances of life itself just as necessary, not only that we may meet the particular problem of the moment truly, but that we may gain all the experience which may be helpful in meeting other difficult circumstances as they present themselves.

We must first convince ourselves thoroughly of the truth that CIRCUMSTANCES, HOWEVER DIFFICULT, ARE ALWAYS—WITHOUT EXCEPTION, OPPORTUNITIES, AND NOT LIMITATIONS.

They are not by any means opportunities for taking us in the direction that our own selfishness would have us go; they are opportunities which are meant to guide us in the direction we most need to follow,—in the ways that will lead us to the greatest strength in the end.

The most unbelieving of us will admit that "there is a destiny which shapes our ends, rough hew them as we may," and it is in the stupid resistance to having our ends shaped for us that we stop and groan at what we call the limitations of circumstances.

If we were quickly alert to see where circumstances had placed the gate of opportunity, and then steadily persisted in going through it, it would save the loss of energy and happiness which results from obstinately beating our heads against a stone wall where there is no gate, and where there never can be a gate.

Probably there is hardly a reader who will not recall a number of cases in which circumstances appear to have been only limitations to him or to his friends; but if he will try with a willing mind to find the gate of opportunity which was not used, he will be surprised to learn that it was wide open all the time, and might have led him into a new and better country.

The other day a little urchin playing in the street got in the way of a horse, and just saved himself from being run over by a quick jump; he threw up his arms and in a most cheerful voice called out, "It's all right, only different!" If the horse had run over him, he might have said the same thing and found his opportunity to more that was good and useful in life through steady patience on his bed. The trouble is that we are not willing to call it *"all right"* unless it is *the same,*—the same in this case meaning whatever may be identical with our own personal ideas of what is "all right." That expressive little bit of slang is full of humor and full of common sense.

If, for instance, when we expect something and are disappointed, we could at once yield out of our resistance and heartily exclaim, "it is all right, only different," how much sooner we should discover the good use in its being different, and how soon we should settle into the sense of its being "all right!" When a circumstance that has seemed to us *all wrong* can be made, through our quiet way of meeting it, to appear all right, only different, it very soon leads to a wholesome content in the new state of affairs or to a change of circumstances to which we can more readily and happily adjust ourselves.

A strong sense of something's being "all right" means a strong sense of willingness that it should be just as it is. With that clear willingness in our hearts in general, we can adjust ourselves to anything in particular,—even to very sudden and unexpected changes. It is carrying along with us a background of powerful non-resistance which we can bring to the front and use actively at a moment's notice.

It seems odd to think of actively using non-resistance, and yet the expression is not as contradictory as it would appear, for the strength of will it takes to attain an habitual attitude of wholesome non-resistance is far beyond the strength of will required to resist unwholesomely. The stronger, the more fixed and immovable the centre, the more free and adaptable are the circumferences of action; and, even though our central principle is fixed and immovable, it must be elastic enough to enable us to change our point of view whenever we find that by so doing we can gain a broader outlook and greater power for use.

To acquire the strength of will for this habitual non-resistance is sometimes a matter of years of practice. We have to compel ourselves to be "willing," over and over again, at each new opportunity; sometimes the opportunities seem to throng us; and this, truly considered, is only a cause for gratitude.

In life the truest winning often comes first under the guise of failure, and it is willingness to accept failure, and intelligence in understanding its causes, and using the acquired knowledge as a means to a higher end, that ultimately brings true success. If we choose, a failure can always be used as a means to an end rather than as a result in itself.

How often do we hear the complaint, "I could do so well if it were not for my circumstances." How many people are held down for a lifetime by the habitual belief in circumstances as limitations, and by ignoring the opportunities which they afford.

"So long as I must live with these people I can never amount to anything." If this complaint could be changed to the resolve: "I will live with these people until I have so adjusted myself to them as to be contented," a source of weakness would be changed into a source of strength. The quiet activity of mind required to adjust ourselves to difficult surroundings gives a zest and interest to life which we can find in no other way, and adds a certain strength to the character which cannot be found elsewhere. It is interesting to observe, too, how often it happens that, when we have adjusted ourselves to difficult circumstances, we are removed to other circumstances which are more in sympathy with our own, thoughts and ways: and sometimes to circumstances which are more difficult still, and require all the strength and wisdom which our previous discipline has taught us.

If we are alive to our own true freedom, we should have an active interest in the necessary warfare of life. For life is a warfare—not of persons, but of principles—and every man who loves his freedom loves to be in the midst of the battle. Our tendencies to selfish discontent are constantly warring against our love of usefulness and service, and he who wishes to enjoy the full activity of freedom must learn to fight and to destroy the tendencies within himself which stand in the way of his own obedience to law. But he needs, for this, the truthful and open spirit which leads to wise self-knowledge; a quiet and a willing spirit, to make the necessary sacrifice of selfish pride. His quiet earnestness will give him the strength to carry out what his clear vision will reveal to him in the light of truth He will keep his head lifted up above his enemies round about him, so that he may steadily watch and clearly see how best to act. After periods of hard fighting the intervals of rest will be full of refreshment, and will always bring new strength for further activity. If, in the battle with difficult circumstances, we are thrown down, we must pick ourselves up with quick decision, and not waste a moment in complaint or discouragement. We should emphasize to ourselves the necessity for picking ourselves up immediately, and going directly on, over and over again,—both for our own benefit, and the benefit of those whom we have the privilege of helping.

In the Japanese training of "Jiu Jitsu," the idea seems to be to drop all subjective resistance, and to continue to drop it, until, through the calmness and clearness of sight that comes from quiet nerves and a free mind, the wrestler can see where to make the fatal stroke. When the right time has arrived, the only effort which is necessary is quick, sharp and conclusive. This wonderful principle is often misused for selfish ends, and in such cases it leads eventually to bondage because, by the successful satisfaction of selfish motives, it strengthens the hold of our selfishness upon us; but, when used in an unselfish spirit, it is an ever-increasing source of strength. In the case of difficult circumstances,—if we cease to resist,—if we accept the facts of life,—if we are willing to be poor, or ill, or disappointed, or to live with people we do not like,—we gain a quietness of nerve and a freedom of mind which clears off the mists around us, so that our eyes may see and recognize the gate of opportunity,—open before us.

It is the law of concentration and relaxation. If we concentrate on being willing, on relaxing until we have dropped every bit of resistance to the circumstances about us, that brings us to a quiet and well-balanced point of view, whence we can see clearly how to take firm and decided action. From such action the re-action is only renewed strength,—never painful and contracting weakness. If we could give up all our selfish desires and resistances, circumstances, however difficult, would have no power whatever to trouble us. To reach such absolute willingness is a long journey, but there is a straight path leading nearer and nearer to the happy freedom which is our goal.

Self-pity is one of the states that interferes most effectually with making the right use of circumstances. To pity one's self is destruction to all possible freedom. If the reader finds himself in the throes of this weakness and is helped through these words to recognize the fact, let him hasten to shun it as he would shun poison, for it is progressively weakening to soul and body. It will take only slight difficulties of any kind to overthrow us, if we are overcome by this temptation.

Imagine a man in the planet Mars wanting to try his fortunes on another planet, and an angel appearing to him with permission to transfer him to the earth.

"But," the angel says, "of course you can have no idea of what the life is upon the new planet unless you are placed in the midst of various circumstances which are more or less common to its inhabitants."

"Certainly," the Martian answers, "I recognize that, and I want to have my experience on this new planet as complete as possible; therefore the more characteristic and difficult my circumstances are the better." Then imagine the interest that man would have, from the moment he was placed on the earth, in working, his way through, and observing his experience as he worked.

His interest would be alive vivid, and strong, from the beginning until he found himself, with earthly experience completed, ready to return to his friends in Mars. He would never lose courage or be in any way disheartened. The more difficult his earthly problem was, the more it would arouse his interest and vigor to solve it. So many people prefer a difficult problem in geometry to an easy one, then why not in life? The difference is that in mathematics the head alone is exercised, and in life the head and the heart are both brought into play, and the first difficulty is to persuade the head and heart to work together. In the visitor from Mars, of course, the heart would be working with the head, and so the whole man would be centred on getting creditably through his experience and home again. If our hearts and heads were together equally concentrated on getting through our experience for the sake of the greater power of use it would bring,—and, if we could trustfully believe in getting home again, that is, in getting established in the current of ordinary spiritual and natural action, then life would be really alive for us, then we should actually get the scent of our true freedom, and, having once had a taste of it, we should have a fresh incentive in achieving it entirely.

There is one important thing to remember in an effort to be free from the bondage of circumstances which will save us from much unnecessary suffering. This has to do with the painful associations which arise from circumstances which are past and over.

A woman, for example, suffered for a year from nervous exhaustion in her head, which was brought on, among other things, by over-excitement in private theatricals. She apparently recovered her health, and, because she was fond of acting, her first activities were turned in that direction. She accepted a part in a play; but as soon as she began to study all her old head symptoms returned, and she was thoroughly frightened, thinking that she might never be able to use her head again. Upon being convinced, however, that all her discomfort came from her own imagination, through the painful associations connected with the study of her part, she returned to her work resolved to ignore them, and the consequence was that the symptoms rapidly disappeared.

Not uncommonly we hear that a person of our acquaintance cannot go to some particular place because of the painful events which occurred there. If the sufferer could only be persuaded that, when such associations are once bravely faced, it takes a very short time for the painful effects to disappear entirely, much unnecessary and prolonged discomfort would be saved.

People have been kept ill for weeks, months and years, through holding on to the brain impression of some painful event.

Whether the painful circumstances are little or great, the law of association is the same and, in any case, the brain impression can be dropped entirely, although it may take time and patience to do it. We must often talk to our brains as if we were talking to another person to eliminate the impressions from old associations. Tell your brain in so many words, without emotion, that the place or the circumstance is nothing, nothing whatever,—it is only your idea about it, and the false association can be changed to a true one.

So must we yield our selfish resistances and be ready to accept every opportunity for growth that circumstances offer; and, at the same time, when the good result is gained, throw off the impression of the pain of the process entirely and forever. Thus may we both live and observe for our own good and that of others; and he who is practising this principle in his daily life can say from his heart:—"Now shall my head be lifted up above mine enemies round about me."

VIII.
Other People

HOWEVER disagreeable other people may be,—however unjust they may be, however true it may be that the wrong is all on their side and not at all on ours,—whatever we may suffer at their hands,—we can only remedy the difficulty by looking first solely to ourselves and our own conduct; and, not until we are entirely free from resentment or resistance of any kind, and not until we are quiet in our own minds with regard to those who may be oppressing or annoying us, should we make any effort to set them right.

This philosophy is sound and absolutely practical,—it never fails; any apparent failure will be due to our own delinquency in applying it; and, if the reader will think of this truth carefully until he feels able to accept it, he will see what true freedom there is in it,—although it may be a long time before he is fully able to carry it out.

How can I remain in any slightest bondage to another when I feel sure that, however wrong he may be, the true cause of my discomfort and oppression is in myself? I am in bondage to myself, and it is to myself that I must look to gain my freedom. If a friend is rude and unkind to me, and I resent the rudeness and resist the unkindness, it is the resentment and resistance that cause me to suffer. I am not suffering for my friend, I am suffering for myself; and I can only gain my freedom by shunning the resentment and resistance as sin against all that is good and true in friendship. When I am free from these things in myself,—when, as far as I am concerned, I am perfectly and entirely willing that my friend should be rude or unjust, then only am I free from him. It is impossible that he should oppress me, if I am willing that he should be unjust or unkind; and the freedom that comes from such strong and willing non-resistance is like the fresh air upon a mountain. Such freedom brings with it also a new understanding of one's friend, and a new ability to serve him.

Unless we live a life of seclusion, most of us have more than one friend, or acquaintance, or enemy, with whom we are brought into constant or occasional contact, and by whom we are made to suffer; not to mention the frequent irritations that may come from people we see only once in our lives. Imagine the joy of being free from all this irritability and oppression; imagine the saving of nervous energy which would accompany such freedom; imagine the possibility of use to others which would be its most helpful result!

If we once catch even the least glimpse of this quiet freedom, we shall not mind if it takes some time to accomplish so desirable a result, and the process of achieving it is deeply interesting.

The difficulty at first is to believe that so far as we are concerned, the cause Of the trouble is entirely within, ourselves. The temptation is to think:—

"How can I help resenting behavior like that! Such selfishness and lack of consideration would be resented by any one."

So any one might resent it, but that is no reason why we should. We are not to make other people's standards our own unless we see that their standards are higher than ours; only then should we change,—not to win the favor of the other people, but because we have recognized the superior value of their standards and are glad to put away what is inferior for what is better. Therefore we can never excuse ourselves for resentment or resistance because other people resent or resist. There can be no possible excuse for resistance to the behavior of others, and it is safe to say that we must *never pit our wills against the wills of other people.* If we want to do right and the other man wants us to do wrong, we must pass by his will, pass under it or over it, but never on any account resist it. There has been more loss of energy, more real harm done, through this futile engagement of two personal wills than can ever be computed, and the freedom consequent upon refusing such contact is great in proportion. Obedience to this law of not pitting our wills against the wills of other people leads to new freedom in all sorts of ways,—in connection with little, everyday questions, as to whether a thing is one color or another, as well as in the great and serious problems of life. If, in an argument, we feel confident that all we want is the truth,—that we do not care whether we or our opponents are in the right, as long as we find the right itself,—then we are free, so far as personal feeling is concerned; especially if, in addition, we are perfectly willing that our opponents should not be convinced, even though the right should ultimately prove to be on our side.

With regard to learning how always to look first to ourselves,—first we must become conscious of our own resentment and resistance, then we must acknowledge it heartily and fully, and then we must go to work firmly and steadily to refuse to harbor it. We must relax out of the tension of our resistance with both soul and body; for of course, the resistance contracts the nerves of our bodies, and, if we relax from the contractions in our bodies, it helps us to gain freedom from resistance in our hearts and minds. The same resistance to the same person or the same ideas may return, in different forms, many times over; but all we have to do is to persist in dropping it as often as it returns, even if it be thousands of times.

No one need be afraid of losing all backbone and becoming a "mush of concession" through the process of dropping useless resistance, for the strength of will required to free ourselves from the habit of pitting one's own will against that of another is much greater than the strength we use when we indulge the habit. The two kinds of strength can no more be compared than the power of natural law can be compared to the lawless efforts of human waywardness. For the will that is pitted against the will of another degenerates into obstinacy, and weakens the character; whereas the will that is used truly to refuse useless resistance increases steadily in strength, and develops power and beauty of character. Again, the man who insists upon pitting his will against that of another is constantly blinded as to the true qualities of his opponent. He sees neither his virtues nor his vices clearly; whereas he who declines the merely personal contest becomes constantly clarified in his views, and so helped toward a loving charity for his opponent,—whatever his faults or difficulties may be,—and to an understanding and love of the good in him, which does not identify him with his faults.

When we resent and resist, and are personally wilful, there is a great big beam in our eye, which we cannot see through, or under, or over,—but, as we gain our freedom from all such resistance, the beam is removed, and we are permitted to see things as they really are, and with a truer sense of proportion, our power of use increases.

When a person is arguing with all the force of personal wilfulness, it is both pleasant and surprising to observe the effect upon him if he begins to feel your perfect willingness that he should believe in his own way, and your willingness to go with him, too, if his way should prove to be right. His violence melts to quietness because you give him nothing to resist. The same happy effect comes from facing any one in anger, without resistance, but with a quiet mind and a loving heart. If the anger does not melt—as it often does—it is modified and weakened, and—as far as we are concerned—it cannot touch or hurt us.

We must remember always that it is not the repression or concealment of resentment and resistance, and forbearing to express them, that can free us from bondage to others; it is overcoming any trace of resentment or resistance within our own hearts and minds. If the resistance is in us, we are just as much in bondage as if we expressed it in our words and actions. If it is in us at all, it must express itself in one way or another,—either in ill-health, or in unhappy states of mind, or in the tension of our bodies. We must also remember that, when we are on the way to freedom from such habits of resistance, we may suffer from them for a long time after we have ceased to act from them. When we are turning steadily away from them, the uncomfortable effects of past resistance may linger for a long while before every vestige of them disappears. It is like the peeling after scarlet fever,—the dead skin stays on until the new, tender skin is strong underneath, and after we think we have peeled entirely, we discover new places with which we must be patient. So, with the old habits of resistance, we must, although turning away from them firmly, be steadily patient while waiting for the pain from them to disappear. It must take time if the work is to be done thoroughly,—but the freedom to be gained is well worth waiting for.

One of the most prevalent forms of bondage is caring too much in the wrong way what people think of us. If a man criticises me I must first look to see whether he is right. He may be partly right, and not entirely,—but, whatever truth there is in his criticism, I want to know it in order that I may see the fault clearly myself and remedy it. If his criticism is ill-natured it is not necessarily any the less true, and I must not let the truth be obscured by his ill-nature. All, that I have to do with the ill-nature is to be sorry, on my friend's account, and help him out of it if he is willing; and there is nothing that is so likely to make him willing as my recognizing the justice of what he says and acting upon it, while, at the same time, I neither resent nor resist his ill-nature. If the man is both ill-natured and unjust,—if there is no touch of what is true in his criticism,—then all I have to do is to cease resenting it. I should be perfectly willing that he should think anything he pleases, while I, so far as I can see, go on and do what is right.

The trouble is that we care more to appear right than to be right. This undue regard for appearances is very deep-seated, for it comes from long habit and inheritance; but we must recognize it and acknowledge it in ourselves, in order to take the true path toward freedom. So long as we are working for appearances we are not working for realities. When we love to *be* right first, then we will regard appearances only enough to protect what is good and true from needless misunderstanding and disrespect. Sometimes we cannot even do that without sacrificing the truth to appearances, and in such cases we must be true to realities first, and know that appearances must harmonize with them in the end. If causes are right, effects must be orderly, even though at times they may not seem so to the superficial observer. Fear of not being approved of is the cause of great nervous strain and waste of energy; for fear is resistance, and we can counteract that terrified resistance only by being perfectly willing that any one should think anything he likes. When moving in obedience to law—natural and spiritual—a man's power cannot be overestimated; but in order to learn genuine obedience to law, we must be willing to accept our limitations and wait for them to be gradually removed as we gain in true freedom. Let us not forget that if we are overpleased—selfishly pleased—at the approval of others, we are just as much in bondage to them as if we were angry at their disapproval. Both approval and disapproval are helpful if we accept them for the use they can be to us, but are equally injurious if we take them to feed our vanity or annoyance.

It is hard to believe, until our new standard is firmly established, that only from this true freedom do we get the most vital sense of loving human intercourse and companionship, for then we find ourselves working hand in hand with those who are united to us in the love of principles, and we are ready to recognize and to draw out the best in every one of those about us.

If this law of freedom from others—which so greatly increases our power of use to them and their power of use to us—had not been proved absolutely practical, it would not be a law at all. It is only as we find it practical in every detail, and as obedience to it is proved to be the only sure road to established freedom that we are bound to accept it. To learn to live in such obedience we must be steady, persistent and patient,—teaching ourselves the same truths many times, until a new habit of freedom is established within us by the experience of our daily lives. We must learn and grow in power from every failure; and we must not dwell with pride and complacency on good results, but always move steadily and quietly forward.

IX.
Human Sympathy

A NURSE who had been only a few weeks in the hospital training-school, once saw—from her seat at the dinner-table—a man brought into the house who was suffering intensely from a very severe accident. The young woman started up to be of what service she could, and when she returned to the table, had lost her appetite entirely, because of her sympathy for the suffering man. She had hardly begun her dinner, and would have gone without it if it had not been for a sharp reprimand from the superintendent.

"If you really sympathize with that man," she said, "you will eat your dinner to get strength to take care of him. Here is a man who will need constant, steady, *healthy* attention for some days to come,—and special care all this afternoon and night, and it will be your duty to look out for him. Your 'sympathy' is already pulling you down and taking away your strength, and you are doing what you can to lose more strength by refusing to eat your dinner. Such sympathy as that is poor stuff; I call it weak sentimentality."

The reprimand was purposely sharp, and, by arousing the anger and indignation of the nurse, it served as a counter-irritant which restored her appetite. After her anger had subsided, she thanked the superintendent with all her heart, and from that day she began to learn the difference between true and false sympathy. It took her some time, however, to get thoroughly established in the habit of healthy sympathy. The tendency to unwholesome sympathy was part of her natural inheritance, along with many other evil tendencies which frequently have to be overcome before a person with a very sensitive nervous system can find his own true strength. But as she watched the useless suffering which resulted in all cases in which people allowed themselves to be weakened by the pain of others, she learned to understand more and more intelligently the practice of wholesome sympathy, and worked until it had become her second nature. Especially did she do this after having proved many times, by practical experience, the strength which comes through the power of wholesome sympathy to those in pain.

Unwholesome sympathy incapacitates one for serving others, whether the need be physical, mental, or moral. Wholesome sympathy not only gives us power to serve, but clears our understanding; and, because of our growing ability to appreciate rightly the point of view of other people, our service can be more and more intelligent.

In contrast to this unwholesome sympathy, which is the cause of more trouble in the world than people generally suppose, is the unwholesome lack of sympathy, or hardening process, which is deliberately cultivated by many people, and which another story will serve to illustrate.

A poor negro was once brought to the hospital very ill; he had suffered so keenly in the process of getting there that the resulting weakness, together with the intense fright at the idea of being in a hospital, which is so common to many of his class, added to the effects of his disease itself, were too much for him, and he died before he had been in bed fifteen minutes. The nurse in charge looked at him and said, in a cold, steady tone:—

"It was hardly worth while to make up the bed."

She had hardened herself because she could not endure the suffering of unwholesome sympathy, and yet "must do her work." No one had taught her the freedom and power of true sympathy. Her finer senses were dulled and atrophied,—she did not know the difference between one human soul and another. She only knew that this was a case of typhoid fever, that a case of pneumonia, and another a case of delirium tremens. They were all one to her, so far as the human beings went. She knew the diagnosis and the care of the physical disease,—and that was all. She did the material work very well, but she must have brought torture to the sensitive mind in many a poor, sick body.

Another form of false sympathy is what may be called professional sympathy. Some people never find that out, but admire and get comfort from the professional sympathy of a doctor or a nurse, or any other person whose profession it is to care for those who are suffering. It takes a keen perception or a quick emergency to bring out the false ring of professional sympathy. But the hardening process that goes on in the professional sympathizer is even greater than in the case of those who do not put on a sympathetic veneer. It seems as if there must be great tension in the more delicate parts of the nervous system in people who have hardened themselves, with or without the veneer,—akin to what there would be in the muscles if a man went about his work with both fists tightly clenched all day, and slept with them clenched all night. If that tension of hard indifference could be reached and relaxed, the result would probably be a nervous collapse, before true, wholesome habits could be established, but unfortunately it often becomes so rigid that a healthy relaxation is out of the question. Professional sympathy is of the same quality as the selfish sympathy which we see constantly about us in men or women who sympathize because the emotion attracts admiration and wins the favor of others.

When people sympathize in their selfishness instead of sympathizing in their efforts to get free, the force of selfishness is increased, and the world is kept down to a lower standard by just so much.

A thief, for instance, fails in a well-planned attempt to get a large sum of money, and confides his attempt and failure to a brother thief, who expresses admiration for the sneaking keenness of the plan, and hearty sympathy in the regret for his failure. The first thief immediately pronounces the second thief "a good fellow." But, at the same time, if either of these apparently friendly thieves could get more money by cheating the other the next day he would not hesitate to do so.

To be truly sympathetic, we should be able so to identify ourselves with the interests of others that we can have a thorough appreciation of their point of view, and can understand their lives clearly, as they appear to themselves; but this we can never do if we are immersed in the fog,—either of their personal selfishness or our own. By understanding others clearly, we can talk in ways that are, and seem to them, rational, and gradually lead them to a higher standard.

If a woman is in the depths of despair because a dress does not fit, I should not help her by telling her the truth about her character, and lecturing her upon her folly in wasting grief upon trifles, when there are so many serious troubles in the world. From her point of view, the fact that her dress does not fit *is* a grief. But if I keep quiet, and let her see that I understand her disappointment, and at the same time hold my own standard, she will be led much more easily and more truly to see for herself the smallness of her attitude. First, perhaps, she will be proud that she has learned not to worry about such a little thing as a new dress; and, if so, I must remember her point of view, and be willing that she should be proud. Then, perhaps, she will come to wonder how she ever could have wasted anxiety on a dress or a hat, and later she may perhaps forget that she ever did.

It is like leading a child. We give loving sympathy to a child when it breaks its doll, although we know there is nothing real to grieve about There is something for the child to grieve about, something very real *to her;* but we can only sympathize helpfully with her point of view by keeping ourselves clearly in the light of our own more mature point of view.

From the top of a mountain you can see into the valley round about,—your horizon is very broad, and you can distinguish the details that it encompasses; but, from the valley, you cannot see the top of the mountain, and your horizon is limited.

This illustrates truly the breadth and power of wholesome human sympathy. With a real love for human nature, if a man has a clear, high standard of his own,—a standard which he does not attribute to his own intelligence—his understanding of the lower standards of other men will also be very clear, and he will take all sorts and conditions of men into the region within the horizon of his mind. Not only that, but he will recognize the fact When the standard of another man is higher than his own, and will be ready to ascend at once when he becomes aware of a higher point of view. On the other hand, when selfishness is sympathizing with selfishness, there is no ascent possible, but only the one little low place limited by the personal, selfish interests of those concerned.

Nobody else's trouble seems worth considering to those who are immersed in their own, or in their selfish sympathy with a friend whom they have chosen to champion. This is especially felt among conventional people, when something happens which disturbs their external habits and standards of life. Sympathy is at once thrown out on the side of conventionality, without any rational inquiry as to the real rights of the case. Selfish respectability is most unwholesome in its unhealthy sympathy with selfish respectability.

The wholesome sympathy of living human hearts sympathizes first with what is wholesome,—especially in those who suffer,—whether it be wholesomeness of soul or body; and true sympathy often knows and recognizes that wholesomeness better than the sufferer himself. Only in a secondary way, and as a means to a higher end, does it sympathize with the painful circumstances or conditions. By keeping our sympathies steadily fixed on the health of a brother or friend, when he is immersed in and overcome by his own pain, we may show him the way out of his pain more truly and more quickly. By keeping our sympathies fixed on the health of a friend's soul, we may lead him out of selfishness which otherwise might gradually destroy him. In both cases our loving care should be truly felt,—and felt as real understanding of the pain or grief suffered in the steps by the way, with an intelligent sense of their true relation to the best interests of the sufferer himself Such wholesome sympathy is alert in all its perceptions to appreciate different points of view, and takes care to speak only in language which is intelligible, and therefore useful. It is full of loving patience, and never forces or persuades, but waits and watches to give help at the right time and in the right place. It is more often helpful with silence than with words. It stimulates one to imagine what friendship might be if it were alive and wholesome to the very core. For, in such friendship as this, a true friend to one man has the capacity of being a true friend to all men, and one who has a thoroughly wholesome sympathy for one human being will have it for all. His general attitude must always be the same—modified only by the relative distance which comes from variety in temperaments.

In order to sympathize with the best possibilities in others, our own standards must be high and clear, and we must be steadily true to them. Such sympathy is freedom itself,—it is warm and glowing,—while the sympathy which adds its weight to the pain or selfishness of others can really be only bondage, however good it may appear.

X.
Personal Independence

IN proportion as every organ of the human body is free to perform its own functions, unimpeded by any other, the body is perfectly healthy and vigorous; and, in proportion as every organ of the body is receiving its proper support from every other, the body as a whole is vigorous, and in the full use of its powers.

These are two self-evident axioms, and, if we think of them quietly for a little while, they will lead us to a clear realization of true personal independence.

The lungs cannot do the work of the heart, but must do their own work, independently and freely; and yet, if the lungs should suddenly say to themselves:

"This is all nonsense,—our depending upon the heart in this way; we must be independent! It is weak to depend upon the other organs of the body!" And if they should repel the blood which the heart pumped into them, with the idea that they could manage the body by themselves, and were not going to be weakly dependent upon the heart, the stomach, or any other organ,—if the lungs should insist upon taking this independent stand, they would very soon stop breathing, the heart would stop beating, the stomach would stop digesting, and the body would die. Or, suppose that the heart should refuse to supply the lungs with the blood necessary to provide oxygen; the same fatal result would of course follow. Or, even let us imagine all the organs of the body agreeing that it is weak to be dependent, and asserting their independence of each other. At the very instant that such an agreement was carried into effect, the body would perish.

Then, on the other hand,—to reverse the illustration,—if the lungs should feel that they could help the heart's work by attending to the circulation of the blood, if the heart should insist that it could inhale and exhale better than the lungs, and should neglect its own work in order to advise and assist the lungs in the breathing, the machinery of the body would be in sad confusion for a time, and would very soon cease altogether.

This imaginary want of real independence in the working of the different organs of the body can be illustrated by the actual action of the muscles. How often we see a man working with his mouth while writing, when he should be only using his hands; or, working uselessly with his left hand, when what he has to do only needs the right! How often we see people trying to listen with their arms and shoulders! Such illustrations might be multiplied indefinitely, and, in all cases, the false sympathy of contraction in the parts of the body which are not needed for the work in hand comes from a wrong dependence,—from the fact that the pats of the body that are not needed, are officiously dependent upon those that are properly active, instead of minding their own affairs and saving energy for their own work.

The wholesome working of the human organism, is so perfect in its analogy to the healthy relations of members of a community, that no reader should pass it by without very careful thought.

John says:—

"I am not going to be dependent upon any man. I am going to live my own life, in my own way, as I expect other men to live theirs. If they will leave me alone, I will leave them alone," and John flatters himself that he is asserting his own strength of personality, that he is emphasizing his individuality. The truth is that John is warping himself every day by his weak dependence upon his own prejudices. He is unwilling to look fairly at another main's opinion for fear of being dependent upon it. He is not only warping himself by his "independence," which is puffed up with the false appearance of strength, but he is robbing his fellow-men; for he cannot refuse to receive from others without putting it out of his own power to give to others. Real giving and receiving must be reciprocal in spirit, and absolutely dependent upon each other.

It is a curious and a sad study to watch the growing slavery of such "independent" people.

James, on the other hand, thinks he cannot do anything without asking another man's advice or getting another man's help; sometimes it is always the same man, sometimes it is one of twenty different men. And so, James is steadily losing the power of looking life in the face, and of judging for himself whether or not to take the advice of others from a rational principle, and of his own free will, and he is gradually becoming a parasite,—an animal which finally loses all its organs from lack of use, so that only its stomach remains,—and has, of course, no intelligence at all. The examples of such men as James are much more numerous than might be supposed. We seldom see them in such flabby dependence upon the will of an individual as would make them conspicuous; but they are about us every day, and in large numbers, in their weak dependence upon public opinion,—their bondage to the desire that other men should think well of them. The human parasites that are daily feeding on social recognition are unconsciously in the process of losing their individuality and their intelligence; and it would be a sad surprise to them if they could see themselves clearly as they really are.

Public opinion is a necessary and true protection to the world as it is, because if it were not for public opinion, many men and women would dare to be more wicked than they are. But that is no reason why intelligent men should order their lives on certain lines just because their neighbors do,—just because it is the custom. If the custom is a good custom, it can be followed intelligently, and because we recognize it as good, but it should not be followed only because our neighbors follow it. Then, if our neighbors follow the custom for the same intelligent reason, it will bring us and them into free and happy sympathy.

Neither should a man hesitate to do right, positively and fearlessly, in the face of the public assertion that he is doing wrong. He should, of course, look himself over many times to be sure that he is doing right, according to his own best light, and he should be willing to change his course of action just as fearlessly if he finds he has made a mistake; but, having once decided, he will respect public opinion much more truly by acting quietly against it with an open mind, than he would if he refused to do right, because he was afraid of what others would think of him. To defy carelessly the opinion of others is false independence, and has in it the elements of fear, however fearless it may seem; but to respectfully ignore it for the sake of what is true, and good, and useful, is sure to enlarge the public heart and to help, it eventually to a clearer charity. Individual dependence and individual independence are absolutely necessary to a well-adjusted balance. It is just as necessary to the individual men of a community as to the individual organs of the body.

It is not uncommon for a person to say:—

"I must give up So-and-so; I must not see so much of him,—I am getting so dependent upon him."

If the apparent dependence on a friend is due to the fact that he has valuable principles to teach which may take time to learn, but which lead in the end to greater freedom, then to give up such companionship, out of regard for the criticism of others would, of course, be weakness and folly itself. It is often our lot to incur the severest blame for the very weaknesses which we have most entirely overcome.

Many people will say:—

"I should rather be independently wrong than dependently right," and others will admire them for the assertion. But the truth is, that whenever one is wrong, one is necessarily dependent, either upon man or devil; but it is impossible to be dependently right, excepting for the comparatively short time that we may need for a definite, useful purpose. If a man is right in his mental and moral attitude merely because his friend is right, and not because he wants the right himself, it will only be a matter of time before his prop is taken away, and he will fall back into his own moral weakness. Of course, a man can begin to be right because his friend is right;—but it is because there is something in him which responds to the good in his friend. Strong men are true to their friendships and convictions, in spite of appearances and the clamor of their critics.

True independence is never afraid of appearing dependent, and true dependence leads always to the most perfect independence.

We cannot, really enjoy our own freedom without the growing desire and power to help other people to theirs. Our own love of independence will bring with it an equal love for the independence of our neighbor; and our own love of true dependence—that is, of receiving wise help from any one through whom it may be sent—will give us an equal love for giving help wherever it will be welcome. Our respect for our own independence will make it impossible that we should insist upon trying to give help to others where it is not wanted; and our own respect for true dependence will give us a loving charity, a true respect for those who are necessarily and temporarily dependent, and teach us to help them to their true balance.

We should learn to keep a margin of reserve for ourselves, and to give the same margin to others. Not to come too near, but to be far enough away from every one to give us a true perspective. There is a sort of familiarity that arises sometimes between friends, or even mere acquaintances, which closes the door to true friendship or to real acquaintance. It does not bring people near to one another, but keeps them apart. It is as if men thought that they could be better friends by bumping their heads together.

Our freedom comes in realizing that all the energy of life should come primarily from a love of principles and not of persons, excepting as persons relate to principles. If one man finds another living on principles that are higher than his own, it means strength and freedom for him to cling to his friend until he has learned to understand and live on those principles himself. Then if he finds his own power for usefulness and his own enjoyment of life increased by his friendship, it would indeed be weak of him to refuse such companionship from fear of being dependent. The surest and strongest basis of freedom in friendship is a common devotion to the same fundamental principles of life; and this insures reciprocal usefulness as well as personal independence. We must remember that the very worst and weakest dependence is not a dependence upon persons, but upon a sin,—whether the sin be fear of public opinion or some other more or less serious form of bondage.

The only true independence is in obedience to law, and if, to gain the habit of such obedience, we need a helping hand, it is truly independent for us to take it.

We all came into the world alone, and we must go out of the world alone, and yet we are exquisitely and beautifully dependent upon one another.

A great German philosopher has said that there should be as much space between the atoms of the body, in relation to its size, as there is between the stars in relation to the size of the universe,—and yet every star is dependent upon every other star,—as every atom in the body is dependent upon every other atom for its true life and action. This principle of balance in the macrocosm and the microcosm is equally applicable to any community of people, whether large or small. The quiet study and appreciation of it will enable us to realize the strength of free dependence and dependent freedom in the relation of persons to one another. The more truly we can help one another in freedom toward the dependence upon law, which is the axis of the universe, the more wholesome and perfect will be all our human relations.

XI.
Self-control

TO most people self-control means the control of appearances and not the control of realities. This is a radical mistake, and must be corrected, if we are to get a clear idea of self-control, and if we are to make a fair start in acquiring it as a permanent habit.

I am what I am by virtue of my own motives of thought and action, by virtue of what my mind is, what my will is, and what I am in the resultant combination of my mind and will; I am not necessarily what I appear from the outside.

If a man is ugly to me, and I want to knock him down, and refrain from doing so simply because it would not appear well, and is not the habit of the people about me, my desire to knock him down is still a part of myself, and I have not controlled myself until I am absolutely free from that interior desire. So long as I am in hatred to another, I am in bondage to my hatred; and if, for the sake of appearances, I do not act or speak from it, I am none the less at its mercy, and it will find an outlet wherever it can do so without debasing me in the eyes of other men more than I am willing to be debased. The control of appearances is merely outward repression, and a very common instance of this may be observed in the effort to control a laugh. If we repress it, it is apt to assert itself in spite of our best efforts; whereas, if we relax our muscles, and let the sensation go through us, we can control our desire to laugh and so get free from it. When we repress a laugh, we are really holding on to it, in our minds, but, when we control it by relaxing the tension that comes from the desire to laugh, it is as if the sensation passed over and away from us.

It is a well-known fact among surgeons that, if a man who is badly frightened, takes ether, no matter how well he controls his outward behavior, no matter how quiet he appears while the ether is being administered, as soon as he loses control of his voluntary muscles, the fear that has been repressed rushes out in the form of excitement. This is a practical illustration of the fact that control of appearances is merely control of the muscles, and that, even so far as our nervous system goes, it is only repression, and self-repression is not self-control.

If I repress the expression of irritability, anger, hatred, or any other form of evil, it is there, in my brain, just the same; and, in one form or another, I am in bondage to it. Sometimes it expresses itself in little meannesses; sometimes it affects my body and makes me ill; often it keeps me from being entirely well. Of one thing we may be sure,—it makes me the instrument of evil, in one way or another. Repressed evil is not going to lie dormant in us forever; it will rise in active ferment, sooner or later. Its ultimate action is just as certain as that a serious impurity of the blood is certain to lead to physical disease, if it is not counteracted.

Knowing this to be true, we can no longer say of certain people "So-and-so has remarkable self-control." We can only say, "So-and-so represses his feelings remarkably well: what a good actor he is!" The men who have real self-control do exist, and they are the leaven that saves the race. It is good to know that this habitual repression comes, in many cases, from want of knowledge of the fact that self-repression is not self-control.

But the reader may say, "what am I to do, if I feel angry, and want to hit a man in the face; I am not supposed to hit him am I, rather than to repress my feelings?"

No, not at all, but you are supposed to use your will to get in behind the desire to hit him, and, by relaxing in mind and body, and stopping all resistance to his action, to remove that desire in yourself entirely. If once you persistently refuse to resist by dropping the anger of your mind and the tension of your body, you have gained an opportunity of helping your brother, if he is willing to be helped; you have cleared the atmosphere of your own mind entirely, so that you can understand his point of view, and give him the benefit of reasonable consideration; or, at the very least, you have yourself ceased to be ruled by his evils, for you can no longer be roused to personal retaliation. It is interesting and enlightening to recognize the fact that we are in bondage to any man to the extent that we permit ourselves to be roused to anger or resentment by his words or actions.

When a man's brain is befogged by the fumes of anger and irritability it can work neither clearly nor quietly, and, when that is the case, it is impossible for him to serve himself or his neighbor to his full ability. If another person has the power to rouse my anger or my irritability, and I allow the anger or the irritability to control me, I am, of course, subservient to my own bad state, and at the mercy of the person who has the power to excite those evil states just in so far as such excitement confuses my brain.

Every one has in him certain inherited and personal tendencies which are obstacles to his freedom of mind and body, and his freedom is limited just in so far as he allows those tendencies to control him. If he controls them by external repression, they are then working havoc within him, no matter how thoroughly he may appear to be master of himself. If he acknowledges his mistaken tendencies fully and willingly and then refuses to act, speak, or think from them, he is taking a straight path toward freedom of life and action.

One great difficulty in the way of self-control is that we do not want to get free from our anger. In such cases we can only want to want to, and if we use the strength of will that is given us to drop our resistance in spite of our desire to be angry we shall be working toward our freedom and our real self-control.

There is always a capacity for unselfish will, the will of the better self, behind the personal selfish will, ready and waiting for us to use it, and it grows with use until finally it overrules the personal selfish will with a higher quality of power. It is only false strength that supports the personal will,—a false appearance of strength which might be called wilfulness and which leads ultimately to the destruction of its owner. Any true observer of human nature will recognize the weakness of mere selfish wilfulness in another, and will keep entirely free from its trammels by refusing to meet it in a spirit of resentment or retaliation.

Real self-control, as compared to repression, is delightful in its physical results, when we have any difficult experience to anticipate or to go through. Take, for instance, a surgical operation. If I control myself by yielding, by relaxing the nervous tension which is the result of MY fear, true self-control then becomes possible, and brings a helpful freedom from, reaction after the trouble is over. Or the same principle can be applied if I have to go through a hard trial with a friend and must control myself for his sake,—dropping resistance in my mind and in my body, dropping resistance to his suffering, yielding my will to the necessities of the situation,—this attitude will leave me much more clear to help him, will show him how to help himself, and will relieve him from the reaction that inevitably follows severe nervous strain. The power of use to others is increased immeasurably when we control ourselves interiorly, and do not merely outwardly repress.

It often happens that a drunkard who is supposed to be "cured," returns to his habit, simply because he has wanted his drink all the time, and has only been taught to repress his appetite; if he had been steadily and carefully taught real self-control, he would have learnt to control and drop his interior *desire,* and thus keep permanently free. How often we see intemperance which had shown itself in drink simply turned into another channel, another form of selfish indulgence, and yet the victim will complacently boast of his self-control. An extreme illustration of this truth is shown in the case of a well-known lecturer on temperance. He had given up drink, but he ate like a glutton, and his thirst for applause was so extreme as to make him appear almost ridiculous when he did not receive it.

The opportunities for self-control are, of course, innumerable; indeed they constitute pretty much the whole of life. We are living in freedom and use, real living use, in proportion as we are in actual control of our selfish selves, and led by our love of useful service. In proportion as we have through true self-control brought ourselves into daily and hourly obedience to law, are we in the freedom that properly belongs to our lives and their true uses.

When once we have won our freedom from resistance, we must use that freedom in action, and put it directly to use. Sometimes it will result in a small action, sometimes in a great one; but, whatever it is, it must be *done.* If we drop the resistance, and do not use the freedom gained thereby for active service, we shall simply react into further bondage, from which it will be still more difficult to escape. Having dropped my antagonism to my most bitter enemy, I must do something to serve him, if I can. If I find that it is impossible to serve him, I can at least be of service to someone else; and this action, if carried out in the true spirit of unselfish service, will go far toward the permanent establishment of my freedom.

If a circumstance which is atrociously wrong in itself makes us indignant, the first thing to do is to drop the resistance of our indignation, and then to do whatever may be within our power to prevent the continuance of such wrong. Many people weaken their powers of service by their own indignation, when, if they would cease their excited resistance, they would see clearly how to remedy the wrong that arouses their antagonism. Action, when accompanied by personal resistance, however effective it may seem, does not begin to have the power that can come from action, without such resistance. As, for instance, when we have to train a child with a perverse will, if we quietly assert what is right to the child, and insist upon obedience without the slightest antagonistic feeling to the child's naughtiness, we accomplish much more toward strengthening the character of the child than if we try to enforce our idea by the use of our personal will, which is filled with resistance toward the child's obstinacy. In the latter case, it is just pitting our will against the will of the child, which is always destructive, however it may appear that we have succeeded in enforcing the child's obedience. The same thing holds true in relation to an older person, with the exception that, with him or her, we cannot even attempt to require obedience. In that case we must,—when it is necessary that we should speak at all,—assert the right without antagonism to what we believe to be their wrong, and without the slightest personal resistance to it. If we follow this course, in most cases our friend will come to the right point of view,—sometimes the result seems almost miraculous,—or, as is often the case, we, because we are wholesomely open-minded, will recognize any mistake in our own point of view, and will gladly modify it to agree with that of our friend.

The trouble is that very few of us feel like working to remedy a wrong merely for the sake of the right, and therefore we must have an impetus of personal feeling to carry us on toward the work of reformation. If we could once be strongly started in obedience to the law from love of the law itself, we should find in that impersonal love a clear light and power for effective action both in the larger and in the smaller questions of life.

There is a popular cry against introspection and an insistence that it is necessarily morbid, which works in direct opposition to true self-control. Introspection for its own sake is self-centred and morbid, but we might as well assert that it is right to have dirty hands so long as we wear gloves, and that it is morbid to want to be sure that our hands are clean under our gloves, as to assert that introspection for the sake of our true spiritual freedom is morbid. If I cannot look at my selfish motives, how am I going to get free from them? It is my selfish motives that prevent true self-control. It is my selfish motives that prompt me to the false control of repression, which is counterfeit and for the sake of appearances alone. We must see these motives, recognize and turn away from them, in order to control ourselves interiorly into line with law. We cannot possibly see them unless we look for them. If we look into ourselves for the sake of freedom, for the sake of our greater power for use, for the sake of our true self-control, what can be more wholesome or what can lead us to a more healthy habit of looking out from ourselves into the lives and interests of others? The farther we get established in motives that are truly unselfish, the sooner we shall get out of our own light, and the wider our horizon will be; and the wider our horizon, the greater our power for use.

There must, of course, be a certain period of self-consciousness in the process of finding our true self-control, but it is for the sake of an end which brings us more and more fully into a state of happy, quiet spontaneity. If we are working carefully for true self-control we shall welcome an unexpected searchlight from another mind. If the searchlight brings into prominence a bit of irritation that we did not know was there, so much the better. How could we free ourselves from it without knowing that it was there? But as soon as we discover it we can control and cast it off. A healthy introspection is merely the use of a searchlight which every one who loves the truth has the privilege of using for the sake of his own growth and wilfulness, and circumstances often turn it full upon us, greatly to our advantage, if we do not wince but act upon the knowledge that it brings. It is possible to acquire an introspective habit which is wholesome and true, and brings us every day a better sense of proportion and a clearer outlook.

With regard to the true control of the Pleasurable emotions, the same principle applies.

People often grow intensely excited in listening to music,—letting their emotions run rampant and suffering in consequence a painful reaction of fatigue. If they would learn to yield so that the music could pass over their nerves as it passes over the strings of a musical instrument, and then, with the new life and vigor derived from the enjoyment, would turn to some useful work, they would find a great expansion in the enjoyment of the music as well as a new pleasure in their work.

Real self-control is the subjugation of selfishness in whatever form it may exist, and its entire subordination to spiritual and natural law. Real self-control is not self-centred. In so far as we become established in this true self-control, we are upheld by law and guided by the power behind it to the perfect freedom and joy of a useful life.

XII.
The Religion of It

THE religion of it is the whole of it. "All religion has relation to life and the life of religion is to do good." If religion does not teach us to do good in the very best way, in the way that is most truly useful to ourselves and to other people, religion is absolutely useless and had better be ignored altogether. We must beware, however, of identifying the idea of religion with the men and the women who pervert it. If an electrician came to us to light our house, and the lights would not burn, we would not immediately condemn all electric lighting as bosh and nonsense, or as sentimental theory; we should know, of course, that this especial electrician did not understand his business, and would at once look about to find a man who did, and get him to put our lights in order. If no electrician really seemed to know his business, and we wanted our lights very much, the next thing to do would be to look into the laws of electricity ourselves, and find out exactly where the trouble was, and so keep at work until we had made our own lights burn, and always felt able, if at any time they failed to burn, to discover and remedy the difficulty ourselves. There is not a man or woman who does not feel, at some time, the need of an inner light to make the path clear in the circumstances of life, and especially in dealing with others. Many men and women feel that need all the time, and happy are those who are not satisfied until the need is supplied and they are working steadily in daily practical life, guided by a light that they know is higher than theory. When the light is once found, and we know the direction in which we wish to travel, the path is not by any means always clear and smooth, it is often, full of hard, rough Places, and there are sometimes miles to go over where our light seems dim; but if we have proved our direction to be right, and keep steadily and strongly moving forward, we are always sure to come into open resting places where we can be quiet, gather strength, and see the light more clearly for the next stage of the journey.

"It is wonderful," some one remarked, "how this theory of non-resistance has helped me; life is quite another thing since I have practised it steadily." The reply was "it is not wonderful when we realize that the Lord meant what He said when He told us not to resist evil." At this suggestion the speaker looked up with surprise and said: "Why, is that in the New Testament? Where, in what part of it?" She never had thought of the sermon on the Mount as a working plan, or, indeed, of the New Testament as a handbook of life,—practical and powerful in every detail. If we once begin to use it daily and hourly as a working plan of life, it is marvellous how the power and the efficiency of it will grow on us, and we shall no more be able to get along without it than an electrician can get along without a knowledge of the laws of electricity.

Some people have taken the New Testament so literally that they have befogged themselves entirely with regard to its real meaning, and have put it aside as impracticable; others have surrounded it with an emotional idea, as something to theorize and rhapsodize about, and have befogged themselves in that way with regard to its real power. Most people are not clear about it because of the tradition that has come to us through generations who have read it and heard it read in church, and never have thought of living it outside. We can have a great deal of church without any religion, but we cannot have religion without true worship, whether the worship is only in our individual souls, or whether it is also the function of a church to which we belong, with a building dedicated to the worship of the Lord to which we go for prayer and for instruction. If we could clear ourselves from the deadening effects of tradition, from sentimentality, from nice theory, and from every touch of emotional and spurious peace, and take up the New Testament as if we were reading it for the first time, and then if we could use it faithfully as a working plan for a time, simply as an experiment,—it would soon cease to be an experiment, and we should not need to be told by any one that it is a divine revelation; we would be confident of that in our own souls. Indeed that is the only way any one can ever be sure of revelation; it must come to each of us alone, as if it had never come to any one before; and yet the beauty and power of it is such that it has come to myriads before us and will come to myriads after us in just the same way.

But there is no real revelation for any one *until he has lived what he sees to be true.* I may talk like an angel and assert with a shining face my confident faith in God and in all His laws, but my words will mean nothing whatever, unless I have so lived my faith that it has been absorbed, into my character and so that the truths of my working plan have become my second nature.

Many people have discovered that the Lord meant what He said when He said: "Resist not evil," and have proved how truly practical is the command, in their efforts to be willing to be ill, to be willing that circumstances should seem to go against them, to be willing that other people should be unjust, angry, or disagreeable. They have seen that in yielding to circumstances or people entirely,—that is, in dropping their own resistances,—they have gained clear, quiet minds, which enables them to see, to understand, and to practise a higher common sense in the affairs of their lives, which leads to their ultimate happiness and freedom. It is now clear to many people that much of the nervous illness of to-day is caused by a prolonged state of resistance to circumstances or to people which has kept the brain in a strained and irritated state so that it can no longer do its work; and that the patient has to lay by for a longer or a shorter period, according to his ability to drop the resistances, and so allay the irritation and let his brain and nervous system rest and heal.

Then with regard to dealing with others, some of us have found out the practical common sense of taking even injustice quietly and without resistance, of looking to our own faults first, and getting quite free from all resentment and resistance to the behavior of others, before we can expect to understand their point of view, or to help them to more reasonable, kindly action if they are in error. Very few of us have recognized and acknowledged that that was what the Lord meant when He said: "Judge not that ye be not judged. For with what judgment ye judge, ye shall be judged: and with what measure ye mete, it shall be measured to you again. And why beholdest thou the mote that is in thy brother's eye, but considerest not the beam that is in thine own eye? Or how wilt thou say to thy brother, Let me pull out the mote out of thine eye; and, behold, a beam is in thine own eye? Thou hypocrite, first cast out the beam out of thine own eye; and then shalt thou see clearly to cast out the mote out of thy brother's eye."

It comes with a flash of recognition that is refreshingly helpful when we think we have discovered a practical truth that works, and then see that it is only another way of putting what has been taught for the last two thousand years.

Many of us understand and appreciate the truth that a man's true character depends upon his real, interior motives. He is only what his motives are, and not, necessarily, what his motives appear to be. We know that, if a man only controls the appearance of anger and hatred, he has no real self-control whatever. He must get free from the anger itself to be free in reality, and to be his own master. We must stop and think, however, to understand that this is just what the Lord meant when He told us to clean the inside of the cup and the platter, and we need to think more to realize the strength of the warning, that we should not be "whitened sepulchres."

We know that we are really related to those who can and do help us to be more useful men and women, and to those whom we can serve in the most genuine way; we know that we are wholesomely dependent upon all from whom we can learn, and we should be glad to have those freely dependent upon us whom we can truly serve. It is most strengthening when we realize that this is the true meaning of the Lord's saying, "For whosoever shall do the will of God, the same is my brother, and my sister, and mother." That the Lord Himself, with all His strength, was willing to be dependent, is shown by the fact that, from the cross, He said to those who had crucified Him, "I thirst." They had condemned Him, and crucified Him, and yet He was willing to ask them for drink, to show His willingness to be served by them, even though He knew they would respond only with a sponge filled with vinegar.

We know that when we are in a hard place, if we do the duty that is before us, and keep steadily at work as well as we can, that the hard problem will get worked through in some way. We know that this is true, for we have proved it over and over; but how many people realize that it is because the Lord meant what He said when He told us: to "take no thought for the morrow, for the morrow will take thought for the things of itself."

I am reasoning from the proof of the law to the law itself.

There is no end to the illustrations that we might find proving the spiritual common sense of the New Testament and, if by working first in that way, we can get through this fog of tradition, of sentimentality, and of religious emotion, and find the living power of the book itself, then we can get a more and more clear comprehension of the laws it teaches, and will, every day, be proving their practical power in all our dealings with life and with people. Whether we are wrestling with nature in scientific work, whether we are working in the fine arts, in the commercial world, in the professional world, or are dealing with nations, it is always the same,—we find our freedom to work fully realized only when we are obedient to law, and it is a wonderful day for any human being when he intelligently recognizes and finds himself getting into the current of the law of the New Testament. The action of that law he sees is real, and everything outside he recognizes as unreal. In the light of the new truth, we see that many things which we have hitherto regarded as essential, are of minor importance in their relation to life itself.

The old lady who said to her friend, "My dear, it is impossible to exaggerate the unimportance of things," had learned what it meant to drop everything that interferes, and must have been truly on her way to the concentration which should be the very central power of all life,—obedience to the two great commandments.

Concentration does not mean straining every nerve and muscle toward obedience, it means *dropping every thing that interferes.* If we drop everything that interferes with our obedience to the two great commandments, and the other laws which are given us all through the New Testament to help us obey, we are steadily dropping all selfish resistance, and all tendency to selfish responsibility; and in that steady effort, we are on the only path which can by any possibility lead us directly to freedom.

XIII.
About Christmas

THERE was once a family who had a guest staying with them; and when they found out that he was to have a birthday during his visit they were all delighted at the idea of celebrating it. Days before—almost weeks before—they began to prepare for the celebration. They cooked and stored a large quantity of good things to eat, and laid in a stock of good things to be cooked and prepared on the happy day. They planned and arranged the most beautiful decorations. They even thought over and made, or selected, little gifts for one another; and the whole house was in hurry and confusion for weeks before the birthday came. Everything else that was to be done was postponed until after the birthday; and, indeed, many important things were neglected.

Finally the birthday came, the rooms were all decorated, the table set, all the little gifts arranged, and the guests from outside of the house had all arrived. Just after the festivities had begun a little child said to its mother: "Mamma, where is the man whose birthday it is—"

"Hush, hush," the mother said, "don't ask questions."

But the child persisted, until finally the mother said: "Well, I am sure I do not know, my dear, but I will ask."

She asked her neighbor, and the neighbor looked surprised and a little puzzled.

"Why," she said, "it is a celebration, we are celebrating his birthday, and he is a guest in the house."

Then the mother got interested and curious herself.

"But where is the guest? Where is the man whose birthday it is?" And, this time she asked one of the family. He looked startled at first, and then inquired of the rest of the family.

"Where is the guest whose birthday it is?" Alas I nobody knew. There they were, all excited and trying to enjoy themselves by celebrating his birthday, and he,—some of them did not even know who he was! He was left out and forgotten!

When they had wondered for a little while they immediately forgot again, and went on with their celebrations,—all except the little child. He slipped out of the room and made up his mind to find the man whose birthday it was, and, finally, after a hard search, he found him upstairs in the attic,—lonely and sick.

He had been asked to leave the guestroom, which he had occupied, and to move upstairs, so as to be out of the way of the preparations for his birthday. Here he had fallen ill, and no one had had time to think of him, excepting one of the humbler servants and this little child. They had all been so busy preparing for his birthday festival that they had forgotten him entirely.

This is the way it is with most of us at Christmas time.

Whenever we think of a friend, or even an acquaintance, we think of his various qualities,—not always in detail, but as forming a general impression which we associate with his name. If it is a friend whom we love and admire, we love, especially on his birthday, to dwell on all that is good and true in his character; and at such times, though he may be miles away in body, we find ourselves living with him every hour of the day, and feel his presence, and, from that feeling, do our daily tasks with the greater satisfaction and joy.

Every one in this part of the world, of course, knows whose birthday we celebrate on the twenty-fifth of December. If we imagine that such a man never really existed, that he was simply an ideal character, and nothing more,—if we were to take Christmas Day as the festival of a noble myth,—the ideal which it represents is so clear, so true, so absolutely practical in the way it is recorded in the book of his life, that it would be a most helpful joy to reflect upon it, and to try and apply its beautiful lessons on the day which would especially recall it to our minds.

Or, let us suppose that such a man really did exist,—a man whose character was transcendently clear and true, quiet, steady, and strong,—a man who was full of warm and tender love for all,—who was constantly doing good to others without the slightest display or self-assertion,—a man who was simple and humble,—who looked the whole world in the face and did what was right,—even though the whole respectable world of his day disapproved of him, and even though this same world attested in the most emphatic manner that he was doing what was dangerous and wicked,—a man with spiritual sight so keen that it was far above and beyond any mere intellectual power,—a sight compared to which, what is commonly known as intellectual keenness is, indeed, as darkness unto light; a man with a loving consideration for others so true and tender that its life was felt by those who merely touched the hem of his garment. Suppose we knew that such a man really did live in this world, and that the record of his life and teachings constitute the most valuable heritage of our race,—what new life it would give us to think of him, especially on his birthday,—to live over, so far as we were able, his qualities as we knew them; and to gain, as a result, new clearness for our own everyday lives. The better we knew the man, the more clearly we could think of him, and the more full our thoughts would be of living, practical suggestions for daily work.

But now just think what it would mean to us if we really knew that this humble, loving man were the Creator of the universe—the very God—who took upon Himself our human nature with all its hereditary imperfections; and, in that human nature met and conquered every temptation that ever was, or ever could be possible to man; thus—by self-conquest—receiving all the divine qualities into his human nature, and bringing them into this world within reach of the hearts and minds of all men, to give light and warmth to their lives, and to enable them to serve each other;—if we could take this view of the man's life and work, with what quiet reverence and joy should we celebrate the twenty-fifth of December as a day set apart to celebrate His birth into the world!

If we ourselves loved a truthful, quiet way of living better than any other way, how would we feel to see our friends preparing to celebrate our birthday with strain, anxiety, and confusion? If we valued a loving consideration for others more than anything else in the world, how would it affect us to see our friends preparing for the festival with a forced sense of the conventional necessity for giving?

> Who gives himself with his gift feeds three,—
> Himself, his hungry neighbor, and Me."

That spirit should be in every Christmas gift throughout Christendom. The most thoughtless man or woman would recognize the truth if they could look at it quietly with due regard for the real meaning of the day. But after having heard and assented to the truth, the thoughtless people would, from force of habit, go on with the same rush and strain.

It is comparatively easy to recognize the truth, but it is quite another thing to habitually recognize your own disobedience to it, and compel yourself to shun that disobedience, and so habitually to obey,—and to obey it is our only means of treating the truth with real respect. When you ask a man, about holiday time, how his wife is, not uncommonly he will say:—

"Oh, she is all tired out getting ready for Christmas."

And how often we hear the boast:—

"I had one hundred Christmas presents to buy, and I am completely worn out with the work of it."

And these very women who are tired and strained with the Christmas work, "put on an expression" and talk with emotion of the beauty of Christmas, and the joy there is in the "Christmas feeling."

Just so every one at the birthday party of the absent guest exclaimed with delight at all the pleasures provided, although the essential spirit of the occasion contradicted directly the qualities of the man whose birthday it was supposed to honor.

How often we may hear women in the railway cars talking over their Christmas shopping:—

"I got so and so for James,—that will do for him, don't you think so?"

And, when her companion answers in the affirmative, she gives a sigh of relief, as if to say, now he is off my mind!

Poor woman, she does not know what it means to give herself with her gift. She is missing one of the essentials of the true joy of Christmas Day. Indeed, if all her gifts are given in that spirit, she is directly contradicting the true spirit of the day. How many of us are unconsciously doing the same thing because of our—habit of regarding Christmas gifts as a matter of conventional obligation.

If we get the spirit of giving because of Him whose birthday it is, we shall love to give, and our hearts will go out with our gifts,—and every gift, whether great or small, will be a thoughtful message of love from one to another. There are now many people, of course, who have this true spirit of Christmas giving, and they are the people who most earnestly wish that they had more. Then there are many more who do not know the spirit of a truly thoughtful gift, but would be glad to know it, if it could once be brought to their attention.

We cannot give in a truly loving spirit if we give in order that we may receive.

We cannot give truly in the spirit of Christmas if we rush and hurry, and feel strained and anxious about our gifts.

We cannot give truly if we give more than we can afford.

People have been known to give nothing, because they could not give something expensive; they have been known to give nothing in order to avoid the trouble of careful and appropriate selection: but to refrain from giving for such reasons is as much against the true spirit of Christmas as is the hurried, excited gift-making of conventionality.

Even now there is joy in the Christmas time, in spite of the rush and hurry and selfishness, and the spirit of those who keep the joy alive by remembering whose birthday it is, serves as leaven all over the world.

First let us remember what Christmas stands for, and then let us try to realize the qualities of the great personality which gave the day its meaning and significance,—let us honor them truly in all our celebrations. If we do this, we shall at the same time be truly honoring the qualities, and respecting the needs of every friend to whom we give, and our gifts, whether great or small, will be full of the spirit of discriminating affection. Let us realize that in order to give truly, we must give soberly and quietly, and let us take an hour or more by ourselves to think over our gifts before we begin to buy or to make them. If we do that the helpful thoughts are sure to come, and new life will come with them.

A wise man has described the difference between heaven and hell by saying that in heaven, every one wants to give all that he has to every one else, and that in hell, every one wants to take away from others all they have. It is the spirit of heaven that belongs to Christmas.

XIV.
To Mothers

MOST mothers know that it is better for the baby to put him into his crib and let him go quietly to sleep by himself, than to rock him to sleep or put him to sleep in his mother's arms.

Most mothers know also the difficulty of getting the baby into the right habit of going to sleep; and the prolonged crying that has to be endured by both mother and baby before the habit is thoroughly established.

Many a mother gets worn out in listening to her crying child, and goes to bed tired and jaded, although she has done nothing but sit still and listen. Many more, after listening and fretting for a while, go and take up the baby, and thus they weaken him as well as their own characters.

A baby who finds out, when he is two months old, that his mother will take him up if he cries, is also apt to discover, if he cries or teases enough, that his mother will let him have his own way for the rest of his life.

The result is that the child rules the mother, rather than the mother the child; and this means sad trouble and disorder for both.

Strong, quiet beginnings are a most valuable help to all good things in life, and if a young mother could begin by learning how to sit quietly and restfully and let her baby cry until he quieted down and went to sleep, she would be laying the foundation for a very happy life with her children.

The first necessity, after having seen that nothing is hurting him and that he really needs nothing, is to be willing that he should cry. A mother can make herself willing by saying over and over to herself, "It is right that he should cry; I want him to cry until he has learned to go to sleep quietly by himself He will be a stronger and a more healthy man for getting into all good habits as a child."

Often the mother's spirit is willing, or wants to be willing, but her nerves rebel if, while she is teaching herself to listen quietly, she will take long, quiet breaths very steadily for some time, and will occupy herself with interesting work, she will find it a great help toward dropping nervous resistance.

Children are much more sensitive than most people know, and readily respond to the mother's state of mind; and even though the mother is in the next room, if she is truly dropping her nervous resistance and tension, the baby will often stop his crying all the sooner, and besides, his mother will feel the good effects of her quiet yielding in her care of the baby all day long. She will be rested instead of tired when the baby has gone to sleep. She will have a more refreshing sleep herself, and she will be able to care for the baby more restfully when they are both awake.

It is a universal rule that the more excited or naughty the children are, the more quiet and clear the mother should be. A mother who realizes this for the first time, and works with herself until she is free from all excited and strained resistance, discovers that it is through her care for her children that she herself has learned how to live. Blessed are the children who have such a mother, and blessed is the mother of those children!

It is resistance—resistance to the naughtiness or disobedience in the child that not only hurts and tires the mother, but interferes with the best growth of the child.

"What!" a mother may say, "should I want my child to be naughty? What a dreadful thing!"

No, we should not want our children to be naughty, but we should be willing that they should be. We should drop resistance to their naughtiness, for that will give us clear, quiet minds to help them out of their troubles.

All vehemence is weak; quiet, clear decision is strong; and the child not only feels the strength of the quiet, decisive action, but he feels the help from his mother's quiet atmosphere which comes with it. If all parents realized fully that the work they do for their children should be done in themselves first, there would soon be a new and wonderful influence perceptible all about us.

The greatest difficulty often comes from the fact that children have inherited the evil tendencies of their parents, which the parents themselves have not acknowledged and overcome. In these cases, most of all, the work to be done for the child must first be done in the parents.

A very poor woman, who was living in one room with her husband and three children, once expressed her delight at having discovered how to manage her children better: "I see!" she said, "the more I hollers, the more the children hollers; now I am not going to holler any more."

There is "hollering" of the voice, and there is "hollering" of the spirit, and children echo and suffer from both.

The same thing is true from the time they are born until they are grown up, when it should be right for them to be their own fathers and mothers, so far as their characters are concerned, that they can receive the greatest possible help from their parents through quiet non-resistance to their naughtiness, combined with firm decision in demanding obedience to law,—a decision which will derive its weight and influence from the fact that the parents themselves obey the laws to which they require obedience.

Thus will the soul of the mother be mother to the soul of her child, and the development of mother and child be happily interdependent.

It is, of course, not resisting to be grieved at the child's naughtiness,—for that grief must come as surely as penitence for our own wrongdoing.

The true dropping of resistance brings with it a sense that the child is only given to us in trust, and an open, loving willingness leaves us free to learn the highest way in which the trust may be fulfilled.